EPPING

DIG IN!

BRENT OWENS
DIG IN!

CLASSIC RECIPES REINVENTED FROM THE WINNER OF **MASTERCHEF**

hardie grant books
MELBOURNE · LONDON

CONTENTS

DIG DEEPER

THE OTHER DAY I GOT TAGGED
IN A FACEBOOK PHOTO. THE
PHOTO WAS TAKEN A COUPLE
OF YEARS AGO AND SHOWS ME
WEARING CHEF'S WHITES THAT
BELONGED TO A FRIEND WHO
WORKS IN CATERING. IN THE
PHOTO I LOOK SO INCREDIBLY
HAPPY – I THINK THAT'S THE
DAY THAT EVERYONE, INCLUDING
ME, REALISED JUST HOW MUCH
I LOVE COOKING.

I don't think anyone in my family knew I
could cook until Christmas last year, when
I cooked lunch single-handed for the extended
family - twenty-odd people. I did the whole
spread and everyone was blown away.

Like most people, I first started cooking
from necessity. I became independent at
sixteen, so I had to learn to fend for myself.
I remember being in year 10 and coming
home from school to cook up some burgers
for lunch. I'd sit down and watch television
during lunch break, and often there happened
to be a cooking show on. It was a gradual
progression from there. I liked watching Jamie

Oliver, then saw there was another show of
his on a cable food channel, so I'd watch that.
Then I'd get involved in the show that came
after it and eventually I was in front of that
food channel for hours every night. Then I'd go
and try out something I'd seen on TV. I pretty
much learned everything from these shows.

I'd always been a fan of *MasterChef* too,
and often thought I'd like to give it a try. For
two or three years I kept saying, 'I'm going to
do that one day.' My family began to believe
that I could do it too and started to encourage
me, saying, 'What's the worst that could
happen?' My girlfriend, Madison, got sick of
me talking about it so we made a pact to both
audition for different reality shows. I filled in
my application and it sat there for weeks. On
the very last day for applications, I thought
'What the hell!' and pressed the send button.

I developed a lot through the *MasterChef*
experience. Before the show, my cooking was
very rustic - big spreads with a range of hearty
dishes and huge portions. But it was quite
rough and ready. Through my time on the
show I learned how to be more intricate and
delicate and how to make food look good on
the plate. I still love making a big spread, but
now it looks more like a show table! I believe
the way you prepare and present food can
change the result completely. If people are
in love with the look of something they're

already engaged and, chances are, they're going to love the flavour even more.

Seeing people enjoy the food I cook is huge for me. I have always loved entertaining for friends and I tend to go overboard. If someone only eats seafood, then I'll put up four seafood dishes for them, not just one – I don't like seeing people disappointed. I have a great memory of that Christmas Day last year, seeing everyone so impressed and enjoying the food. It was an amazing feeling.

I would describe my cooking as generous. I love everyone sharing dishes or preparing the components so each person can build their own taco or whatever. I also love the element of surprise – to put things in dishes that people wouldn't really expect.

Before *MasterChef*, because I was used to cooking Thai and Mexican food at home, I had already learned a little about balancing flavours, but through being on the show I learned a lot more about how to balance and rebalance. A lot of people think that if you follow a recipe and put everything in a pot and cook it, at the end the flavour will always be the same. But it's not like that. You need to taste, taste, taste and, if something is out, you need to bring it back. All it takes is a little bit of knowledge and practice.

I am way more experimental and creative since *MasterChef*. I invent new dishes and reinvent classics. I think about different tastes – about acidity, bitterness, sweetness and saltiness – in everything I do. I also try to incorporate contrasts of texture and flavour, as well as colour and shape. I play with ingredients and try to do something a little bit unexpected – like working out creative ways to use simple ingredients like barley, or getting a cauliflower and thinking of five different ways I can use it in the same dish.

But because I've eaten a lot of fine food since winning *MasterChef*, I've started to crave what I love best – hearty home-cooked dishes. This is my favourite kind of food, as it triggers memories for me. It's what I ate while growing up and what I first fell in love with.

In this book I have included many classic recipes that I make all the time, which I have reinvented or added a bit of a twist to. They're hearty dishes, usually with robust, memorable flavours. Although there are also some more sophisticated dishes in the book, I believe these are achievable by any home cook. Just give everything a go – making your own pastry, pizza dough, curry pastes, pickles, sauces and smoking food. It's not that hard and each time you do it, it gets easier. It's so worth it, as the satisfaction you get from doing it yourself and seeing people enjoy it, is just awesome.

KITCH
ESSENTIA

You don't need to be the chef of a three-hatted restaurant to cook well. A lot of great chefs use the same techniques that you would use in your own home kitchen every day. The difference is, chefs just become very good at these techniques because they practise them all the time.

Before going on *MasterChef* I didn't have a lot of tips and tricks but, while on the show, I picked up things from other contestants, from the judges and from doing a little bit of reading. I realised I needed to build on my base techniques to broaden my range. Learning little ratios and formulas and perfecting a few basic recipes helped a lot too.

You can simply read a recipe and cook it and not think about it too deeply, but when you understand the building blocks of food and cooking – why you cook ingredients a certain way, and why things like resting meat are important – that's when cooking becomes fun. That's when you can start being creative.

This chapter contains a few guidelines and tips to help you cook better, get the best flavour from your food and to present your dishes well. I've also included a few of my favourite basic recipes that I use all the time.

GET THE BEST FLAVOUR FROM YOUR VEGGIES

There's so much more that you can do with vegetables other than just boiling or steaming them. Think different! Here are a few ideas that you can incorporate into your everyday cooking to get the best from your veg.

ROAST IT

There are so many vegetables that you can roast. Roasting generally brings out the sweetness in a vegetable. You can roast carrots, beetroot, pumpkins, parsnips, cauliflower (it goes nutty), potatoes, Jerusalem artichokes, garlic, sweet potatoes, capsicums, onions and tomatoes. Try them all out. Simply drizzle with a little olive oil and, for extra dimension, add a few bruised garlic cloves, a couple of sprigs of herbs (like thyme, rosemary or sage) and even a sprinkle of spice, such as cumin, smoked paprika (my personal favourite) or an interesting spice blend like Moroccan ras el hanout.

SMOKE IT

You can smoke just about anything, even vegetables. There are two types of smoking – hot and cold. See page 17 for some guidelines and see also my Smoked tomato relish on page 32.

PICKLE IT

There are so many different pickling solutions. I work from a basic one-third water, one-third vinegar (generally apple cider vinegar or red wine vinegar) and one-third white sugar. I bring the mixture to the boil then remove the saucepan from the heat, add the ingredient and leave it to cool down and pickle in the liquid. Pickles add a delicious acidic punch to a dish, which really helps when you have a lot of rich flavours. You'll find I've used this technique a few times in the recipes in this book.

CURRY IT

We don't need meat every night. Have a 'meat-free Monday' and make a delicious curry from pumpkin, sweet potato, eggplant, tomato, cauliflower, potato or sweet potato.

SWEETEN IT

Modern desserts often include savoury vegetables – beetroot, parsnip, pumpkin and carrot are favourites. Slow roasting brings out the sweetness in these ingredients and, paired with sweet elements and salt, they make a delicious, almost savoury dessert. You generally need to purée, or at least roughly mash, the vegetables before using them. Try adding grated carrot or pumpkin to cupcakes or grated beetroot or zucchini to chocolate desserts.

PERFECT VEGETABLE PURÉES

Purées and creams are used often in recipes, especially in restaurants. Do you ever wonder why the ones you eat when you're out taste so great and have so much flavour? It's pretty simple, really:

- Cook the ingredient in its own juice – instead of using stock for cooking carrots, juice a carrot and cook the carrot in the juice before puréeing. This method really accentuates the flavour of the ingredient in the final purée.

- Start with a base. Generally for purées I make with mains, I start with an eschalot (French shallot) and garlic base. See the base recipe below.

BASIC VEGETABLE PURÉE

SERVES 4

2 tablespoons olive oil
2 garlic cloves, finely chopped
2 large eschalots (French shallots), finely chopped
about 600 g of the vegetable to be puréed, grated
60 ml (¼ cup) vegetable stock
60 ml (¼ cup) milk

There are many vegetables that are suitable for serving as a purée. I like to use cauliflower, celeriac, Jerusalem artichoke, pumpkin or carrot.

Heat the oil in a medium saucepan over medium heat. Sweat the garlic and eschalots for a few minutes without colouring. Add your grated vegetable to the pan with the stock. Give it a good stir and cover the pan. It's very important to have the lid on because every bit of steam that leaves the pan means less flavour you'll have in your purée. Cook the vegetable for 12–14 minutes on medium–low heat. You don't want to cook the hell out of the ingredient – you want it cooked, not cremated.

Transfer the slightly cooled mixture to a blender or food processor. I tend to just use a hand-held blender for my purées – it's effective and saves on washing up. Add the milk, season with salt and pepper and blitz until you have a purée of your desired smoothness. Check the seasoning again.

If your purée is a little lumpy, pass it through a fine sieve to ensure silky smoothness.

For a richer result, whack a little butter in there too – butter makes everything taste good!

MAKE YOUR OWN DIPS

It's so easy to make your own dips. Just grab almost anything from the pantry that you think works together and blitz it all together. Think of flavours you love, things that work together and Bob's your uncle!

1 First choose a base – something that has bulk, like a vegetable you can cook and purée (such as pumpkin, eggplant or sweet potato), a tin of your favourite beans or lentils (such as cannellini beans, chickpeas or brown lentils) or a lovely ripe avocado.

2 Add some flavour – lightly sautéed eschalots (French shallots) and garlic are always a great start. Add a touch of spice for impact and fresh herbs for freshness.

3 Balance with a splash of acidity – lemon juice, lime juice or your favourite vinegar (red wine, sherry or champagne vinegar). Season to taste.

4 Swirl through some cream – yoghurt, sour cream, crème fraîche or maybe mascarpone for something a little richer and creamier.

5 Finally top with some texture, some crunch – toasted nuts or seeds or dukkah.

Think beyond opening a packet of dry bikkies when serving your deliciously fresh homemade dips. Instead of crackers from the supermarket, try the following:

- Fresh tortillas or pitta bread cut into long thin wedges – or take them a step further and bake in a 180°C oven for 5–8 minutes until crisp

- Thinly sliced sourdough baguette (toasted or chargrilled if you like)

- Breadsticks (grissini)

- Baby vegetables

- Vegetable sticks – cucumber, red and yellow capsicum, celery, baby carrots, or even raw or blanched broccoli or broccolini

THE BEST WAY TO ROAST A CHICKEN

I don't think I've ever had a perfect whole roast chicken. Why? Because most people don't realise that the legs and the breasts take different times to cook. Whenever I have roast chicken, I separate the legs from the carcass and roast the breasts 'on the crown'. Here are the steps to make perfect roast chicken.

FOR A 1.8 KG CHICKEN
Preheat the oven to 200°C (or 180°C for a fan-forced oven).

Season the chicken skin with salt and freshly ground black pepper and 2 teaspoons of olive oil.

Heat a large ovenproof frying pan or heavy-based roasting tin over high heat. Once the tin is hot, add the chicken legs to start caramelising. Once one side is golden brown, add the carcass, breast side down. Cook over high heat until golden brown all over, about 10 minutes, then place in the oven, breast side up, to roast for 30 minutes, until almost cooked.

Remove the tin from the oven and place it back over high heat. Add 50 g butter and baste the breast and legs for 2–3 minutes.

Place the chicken, upside down, in a bowl covered loosely with foil, to rest for at least 20 minutes.

THE BEST WAY TO POACH A CHICKEN

500 ml (2 cups) chicken stock
offcuts of 2 carrots
offcuts of 2 celery stalks
2 bay leaves
5 peppercorns
salt to taste

It's simple to poach a chicken without thermometers and timers. You need to use chicken stock for the poaching liquid, then build on the flavours. The more you add to the liquid, the more flavour you get in your chicken. I generally poach a chicken breast on the bone and with the skin on. You can poach a skinless breast fillet if you want, but do it gently.

FOR A 200 G CHICKEN BREAST, BONE IN, SKIN ON
Place all the ingredients in a medium saucepan, including the chicken breast, ensuring the chicken is just covered in liquid. Turn on the heat to medium, wait for the liquid to start simmering, then turn it off and let the chicken cool down in the stock. The chicken should be cooked in about 30 minutes, but the longer it cools in the liquid the better.

Remove the chicken from the stock and discard the skin. Perfect! Your left-over stock will make a perfect base for soup.

COOKING WITH MEAT

Cooking red meat sometimes scares people, but it's really not that difficult. If you understand what cut of meat you're using, then you're halfway there.

A prime cut such as beef rib eye, has less fat throughout and therefore has a little less flavour. It's lean and it's quick-cooking, but it's as expensive as hell! Tougher cuts, which are cheaper, have soooo much more flavour. Long braising is the best way to tenderise cheaper cuts, but it's well worth it for the melt-in-your-mouth texture.

CHECKING FOR DONENESS

To keep meat moist and juicy, it should be pink in the centre once cooked. You want red meat to stay below 60°C but above 55°C. If you don't have a thermometer, you can use the hand trick. Hold out the palm of your hand and press on the pad of flesh below the thumb. It feels soft like raw meat. If you touch your thumb together with the tip of your little finger on the same hand and press on the pad, it feels hard, like well-done meat. If you touch your thumb with your ring finger, the pad feels like medium meat. Touching your middle finger and thumb together makes the pad feel like medium-rare and touching your first finger and thumb together makes the pad feel like rare meat.

RESTING

It's vital to rest any meat after cooking. The rule is, whatever the cooking time, rest it for at least half that time (plus about 30 minutes for large roasts). Resting allows the meat fibres to 'relax'. If you cut a piece of meat without resting, the juices will run away. If you allow it to relax, most of the juices will be retained and your meat will be juicier, more tender and flavoursome.

COOKING WITH FISH

There's no bigger showstopper than serving a whole fish at a dinner party. Not only does it look great, but it tastes amazing. Cooking fish on the bone gives it more flavour, keeps it juicier and it has a completely different texture from a fish fillet. Once you've made fish on the bone, you'll cook it again and again.

CHECKING FOR DONENESS

Cooking a whole fish can be intimidating if you don't know how to do it. But the simple truth of testing it is that you unwrap the fish, move a bit of the flesh and see if it's cooked. Don't just take it out of the oven, leave it covered and hope that it's cooked – check it. The best ways to see if a whole fish is cooked are by pushing the flesh away on the thickest part of the fish to see if it's opaque and cooked, or by looking at the fish's eyes, which should be white and slightly sunk into the socket. Also remember that fish will continue to cook for at least 2–3 minutes after being removed from the heat source. I recommend you remove your fish just before it's done and let it rest for a few minutes to be perfectly cooked through.

CRISPY SKIN

Fish fillets, such as snapper, rockling or salmon, are best when they have crispy skin. If they don't then part of the eating experience is incomplete. For crispy skin, salt the skin and cook the fish skin side down, in a little olive oil, for three-quarters of the cooking time. Rest the fish with the skin side up and exposed. When serving, don't cover the skin with anything like a sauce, as the skin will go rubbery again.

SMOKING FOOD

Now this is a favourite technique of mine. You can smoke anything from a carrot to a piece of fish. Smoking meat adds depth of flavour. Delicate meats like salmon will need less time than a rack of pork ribs or a piece of steak. You don't want to oversmoke food though, or the flavour will be overpowering. There are two types of smoking - cold and hot.

COLD SMOKING

With this method you smoke the ingredient before cooking. You do this with a smoking gun (available from kitchen supply stores), which adds the smoke flavour without having to cook the ingredient in smoke.

HOT SMOKING

This is the wok method, which actually cooks the ingredient in the smoke. It doesn't just impart a smoky flavour, it cooks the ingredient too. You need to be careful with this method because it's easy to oversmoke an element, which can overpower your dish.

For hot smoking, line a wok with foil, add your soaked smoking chips or fine smoking sawdust to the bottom along with any whole spices or flavourings that you want. I generally use about 1 cup of smoking chips. I like to add fresh tea leaves to the mix, along with whole spices such as cinnamon sticks, cloves and peppercorns for a bit of an Indian twist. Cover the wok with a lid until smoking, then add your ingredient on a rack 4–5 cm above the smoking mixture to smoke for 3–4 minutes. Check the flavour – if it's not quite smoky enough, smoke it a little longer.

THE ART OF REINVENTION

I've always loved reinventing classic dishes. I like to think of a dish and look at the flavour profile and how I can mix it up. I also think about how it's traditionally cooked and served, then I work out how I might change it, add some surprise elements and take it to a whole new level.

Think about an old-fashioned favourite like the '80s apricot chicken, for instance. How could you transform it from being a simple stew to something new and exciting? Apricots and chicken would be nice together if they were cold, so why not make the apricot into a cold jelly, have the chicken shredded and then make it into a salad? Then think about what else might go with those flavours – maybe a spice such as cinnamon, cloves or cumin. This is now heading down the Middle Eastern route, so think about that cuisine and its ingredients and flavours. Maybe incorporate some couscous, mint or flat-leaf parsley. Next consider some surprise element in the form of texture – add some crunch from pistachio nuts or some sour pops from pomegranate seeds. You've added different elements, different textures and different cooking methods, but it's all based around the original concept of apricot chicken.

When I think about adding a twist to a dish, I look at the main ingredient and think about three or four different cuisines that use that ingredient and the other flavours used in those cusines. Chances are those other flavours will go with your ingredient and you can build a new and exciting dish. For example, I grew up eating a simple Italian chicken cacciatore that was pretty much just chicken and tomato purée. But when I come to cook it, I think of Italian food filled with flavours of garlic, tomato, pancetta, capers, anchovies, parmesan and basil and I try to incorporate a few of those in the dish. Or here's another example that's a bit more out there. Think about blue cheese. The main time people eat blue cheese is on a cheese platter with walnuts, pear or prosciutto. So why not take all of those ingredients and create a dish?

Whenever I construct a dish, I want it to be special the whole way through. I like people to be surprised. I often don't just include one element, but seven or eight – there are surprises here, there and everywhere. You can do this with the simplest of foods. Take a cauliflower. Most people would either boil it or steam it. But why not think of a few different ways of serving it, within the same dish! Maybe think of a base creamy element like a purée or cream and use part of the cauli for that. Then consider roasting some of the small florets in the oven to introduce some nuttiness. Or finely shave some and have it raw for a crunchy element. You could even smoke a little of it and use the outer leaves for presentation.

Think outside the box and make people ask, 'What is that delicious flavour?' when they're eating your food. When people are interested, they will want to know more and taste more and they will enjoy the meal more.

PLATING FOOD

We might 'eat with our eyes', but plating food well is important, not just for appearance, but because if you don't do it right, it can throw out the proportions in the dish. A lot of the recipes I create are based on contrasts of textures and flavours. If something is out of proportion when I serve it up, the whole dish is out. Good plating can also help to change people's perception of a humble dish. I cook a lot of barbecued meat and classic comfort food, but give a simple stew the same treatment as a fine dining dish and people enjoy it even more.

When I start a new dish and before I begin cutting up all the ingredients, I think about how I'm going to present it on the plate at the end. I think about shape, height, textural differences and, most importantly, colour contrast. I start with the main element of my dish in the centre, and then build around that. Don't put anything on a plate that's not there for a reason. Sometimes less is more.

Try to mix up the shapes of the various elements in the dish. If you have a carrot and you already have other finger-shaped or disc-shaped things in the dish, cut the carrot into a cube instead. Try different ways of cutting things, such as shaving or small dicing. Make every bite different.

If you have a straight slice of meat, for example pork, and you're serving it with a purée, sit the pork on a circular pool of the purée or run a strip of purée either side of the meat. If you have a rich sticky sauce, don't just pour it over the top. Pour a little bit here and there in the gaps in the dish, or put a few drops decoratively in a line up the side of the plate. But remember that if you want to have leftovers to use for another dish, don't serve meat on a bed of mashed potato or something similar. You won't be able to keep it if it's covered in mash. Keep the mash or sauce separate.

>

continued from page 19

Not everyone has a range of plates, so if you only have round plates try not to always present your dish in round shapes as it can look boring. If you have a steak or a beef cheek that's round and you have a round plate, slice the meat into strips and lay it across the plate. A lot of the dishes I serve on round plates I arrange in a straight line, sometimes running from one side of the plate to the other – rather than clumping everything in the centre. Contrasts are at the heart of good plating.

You need to think about how people are going to eat the dish, too. Sometimes it's good to decide if you want people to eat things with a knife and fork or just a fork. If you've got a risotto and you have poached chicken on top, slice the chicken into small cubes so it's not out of proportion with the rice and you can eat the whole thing with just a fork if you want to. Also, if you've got a slab of tuna half the size of the plate, you've got to have enough ingredients so that in every mouthful you get a bit of everything. You don't want to have three mouthfuls of tuna and then all the other ingredients are gone and all you have left is the plain tuna.

Garnishes can help add a surprise element and often some texture. It doesn't take much to jazz up a piece of fennel or some parsley. Fry fennel fronds or parsley first and scatter them over the finished dish. Add some little pops of colour and tang with pomegranate seeds. Micro herbs make a great garnish for both savoury and sweet dishes. Why not crumble some cake over a mousse or pudding instead of serving it traditionally in a slice?

Serve food on wooden boards, in glassware, on tiles, still in the pan it was cooked in or on baking paper for easy clean up. Once I served a dip on an upside-down roasting tray as it added height to the spread on the table and it was also handy for people to reach it and dip their bread in. Put desserts in glasses and drinks in jam jars. I love the rustic look of serving a barbecued steak on the board you rested it on. It's runny with juices, but it's so appetising. You don't need expensive crockery – just go get a beautiful piece of wood and cure it.

Don't ever feel scared of trying something new. It doesn't take much to add a point of difference, but it can really improve your dish. It's in those moments of experimentation, of trial and error, that you'll achieve brilliance. What's the worst that can happen?

QUICK WHOLE EGG MAYO...
AND HOW TO SPICE IT UP

**MAKES ABOUT 340 G
(1⅓ CUPS)**

1 large egg
1 teaspoon dijon mustard
1 tablespoon lemon juice
pinch of salt
250 ml (1 cup) oil (blend of
    80 ml/⅓ cup olive oil and
    170 ml/⅔ cup vegetable oil
    works well)

Making your own mayonnaise is so simple. You can add pretty much whatever flavour you desire to the mayo, and below are a few ideas. Mayo is great for spreading on burgers and sandwiches or using as a dipping sauce for chips, vegetables or seafood. Get creative and try out a few of your own ideas.

In a small food processor, pulse the egg, mustard, lemon juice and salt until combined. With the processor running, add the oil gradually in a slow steady stream, until the mayonnaise is the desired consistency. Check for seasoning. Store in an airtight container in the refrigerator for up to 3 days. For flavour variations see below.

VARIATIONS

Lemon and basil mayo

Blitz through the zest of 1 lemon and 30 g (½ cup) finely shredded basil. This is great with seafood.

Parsley mayo

Blitz through 15 g (½ cup) finely chopped flat-leaf parsley. This is great with fish or oven-roasted chips.

Chipotle mayo

Blitz 2–3 tinned chipotle chillies in adobo sauce then fold them through the mayo. This is crazy awesome on a burger.

CREAMY MASH

SERVES 4

5 large floury potatoes,
   peeled and quartered
50 g unsalted butter
white pepper
80 ml (⅓ cup) full cream milk

Don't be freaked out by the amount of butter in this mash.
It's rich and indulgent, the way mash is supposed to be!

In a large saucepan over high heat, bring 750 ml (3 cups) salted
water to the boil. Add the potatoes and cook until tender, about
15 minutes. Strain the potatoes then return them to the saucepan.
Add the butter and, using a masher, mash the potatoes until the
butter is melted and combined. Season with salt and white pepper.
Slowly add the milk and continue to mash until the mixture is
smooth and the desired consistency.

PERFECT CHIPS

SERVES 4

2 floury potatoes, peeled and
   cut into 2 cm x 8 cm chips
500 ml (2 cups) chicken stock
vegetable oil for deep-frying

ROSEMARY SALT
leaves from 2 rosemary sprigs,
   finely chopped
1 tablespoon salt

Whether you're five or fifty, everyone loves chips. These chips
are super-crunchy on the outside and pillow-soft on the inside.

For the rosemary salt, crush the rosemary leaves and salt using a
mortar and pestle to form a coarse salt. Set aside.

Soak the chips in cold water for a few hours to remove some starch.
Drain and pat dry. In a saucepan over high heat, bring the stock to the
boil. Put the chips in a steamer basket over the saucepan, cover and
cook for 8–10 minutes. Remove the chips from the heat and shake
them up a little to roughen the edges. Transfer to a plate lined with
paper towel and place in the refrigerator to cool for 20–30 minutes.

Fill a saucepan one-third full with the vegetable oil and set over
high heat. The oil is hot enough when it bubbles around the handle
of a wooden spoon. Alternatively, turn on a deep-fryer to 180°C.
Add the chips and cook for 5 minutes. Transfer the chips to fresh
paper towel to absorb any excess oil. Reheat the oil in the saucepan
or deep-fryer to 190°C. (If you don't have a themometer use the
wooden spoon trick but just heat the oil a little longer.) Return the
chips to the pan and cook until golden brown and crispy, about
2–3 minutes. Season with the rosemary salt immediately and serve.

TORTILLAS

MAKES 8

2 cups (300 g) plain flour,
plus extra for kneading
1 teaspoon baking powder
½ teaspoon salt
2 tablespoons sunflower oil
150 ml warm water
(approximately)

You can buy tortillas ready made, but they taste so much better if you make your own. It's not that difficult and with a little practice you'll be whipping up fresh tortillas in no time.

Sift the flour, baking powder and salt into a bowl. Make a well in the centre and add the oil and water. Mix until combined. You should have a very soft dough. Cover and set aside to rest for 10 minutes.

Turn the dough out onto a lightly floured surface and knead for 1–2 minutes or until quite smooth. (Don't worry if it's not elastic yet.) Divide the dough into 8 equal-sized balls. Place them in a single layer on a tray lined with baking paper. Cover with plastic wrap and set aside to rest for a further 15 minutes.

Roll out one piece of dough on a lightly floured surface, with a lightly floured rolling pin, very thinly into a circle about 22 cm in diameter. Repeat with the remaining dough balls. (Do not stack the uncooked dough circles on each other or they will stick together.)

Heat a large non-stick frying pan over medium–high heat. When the frying pan is very hot, place a tortilla in the pan and cook for about 1 minute or until lightly browned in places and starting to bubble. Flip and cook the other side for about 30 seconds until slightly puffy, with small golden brown spots on the surface. Do not overcook. Remove the tortillas from the pan and stack them on a plate, covered with a clean tea towel to stop them from drying out and to keep them warm. Repeat the process until they are all done. Serve immediately, or reheat the tortillas briefly in a warm frying pan just before serving.

KIMCHI

1 large (about 1.5 kg) Chinese
    cabbage (wombok)
250 g (1 cup) salt
90 g (½ cup) rice flour
55 g (¼ cup) caster sugar
2 onions, peeled and roughly
    chopped
1 garlic bulb, cloves separated
    and peeled
5 cm piece ginger, peeled and
    roughly chopped
190 ml (¾ cup) fish sauce
100 g (1 cup) kochugaru
    (Korean chilli/red pepper
    powder)
7 spring onions, thinly sliced
1 daikon (white radish),
    peeled and julienned
1 nashi pear, peeled and
    julienned

I love pickles and especially hot and sour kimchi. It's great by itself with rice, in a roll for lunch, as a salad or side with barbecued meat, with teriyaki or with pork buns. This recipe makes a lot, but you will eat it by the fork-load!

Cut the cabbage into quarters and remove the core. Slice the quarters into 4 cm chunks. Rinse well to remove any grit. Put the cabbage in a large bowl, sprinkle with the salt and mix well. Leave for 3 hours, tossing the cabbage every hour. Rinse the cabbage thoroughly several times and set aside to drain in a colander.

Place 625 ml (2½ cups) water in a medium saucepan over medium heat. Add the rice flour, bring to the boil and cook, stirring continuously, for 5–7 minutes until thickened. Add the sugar and cook for a further 2–3 minutes until the sugar dissolves. Remove from the heat and allow to cool.

In a food processor, blitz the onion, garlic and ginger until you have a paste. Add the fish sauce and pulse a few times to combine. Put the paste in a large bowl with the rice flour mixture. Stir in the kochugaru and add the spring onion, daikon, nashi pear and cabbage. Mix thoroughly. Place in a large airtight container and store in the refrigerator.

Check your kimchi after a few days. Bubbles should be forming around the top, which means it is fermenting. If you want to speed up the fermentation process, leave the kimchi out of the refrigerator until it has reached the level of sourness to your taste. Kimchi will keep in the refrigerator, in a sealed container, for several months – if it lasts that long!

BRENT'S TIPS: When you add the paste, it's a good idea to wear disposable gloves and mix it with your hands.

If you're planning on using the kimchi sooner rather than later, leave a small amount out at room temperature to start fermenting quicker than the rest. It might be ready in 3–4 days this way.

JERK SPICE RUB

**MAKES ABOUT 400 G
(1½ CUPS)**

1 small brown onion,
  roughly chopped
5 spring onions, roughly
  chopped
4 garlic cloves, peeled
3 cm piece ginger, roughly
  chopped
5 thyme sprigs, leaves picked
115 g (½ cup) firmly packed
  brown sugar
2–5 habanero chillies
  (depending on how hot you
  like it), roughly chopped
1 teaspoon ground allspice
½ teaspoon ground cinnamon
½ teaspoon ground nutmeg
2–3 tablespoons soy sauce
good pinch of salt and pepper
juice of 1 lime

This African-influenced spice rub is pretty hot. I love it
because the flavours are so different. It's probably like nothing
you've eaten before. There are no unusual ingredients, but
the combination is amazing. It has a lot of power and adds so
much to a dish. Use it with all barbecued meats, but be careful
because the high sugar content means it can burn easily.

Place all the ingredients in a food processor or blender and blitz
until you have a fine paste. Taste and check for seasoning and heat
levels and adjust as necessary. Transfer to a sterilised sealable jar
ready for use. Keeps for 2–3 weeks in the refrigerator.

BRENT'S TIPS: If you think the balance is a little out for your palate,
adjust with a little more of something. If it's too sweet, add more salt;
if too hot, add more sugar, if too salty, add more sugar or chilli. Taste,
taste, taste!

If you can't get your hands on habanero chillies, substitute with
5–7 small red chillies.

THAI CHILLI JAM

MAKES ABOUT 300 G

220 g (1 cup) sugar
10 long red chillies, roughly chopped
2 eschalots (French shallots), roughly chopped
3 garlic cloves, roughly chopped
60 ml (¼ cup) fish sauce
juice of 3 limes
1 teaspoon tamarind purée

Although there's a lot of sugar in this jam to counteract the heat, the flavour comes out well balanced. If you want to make it less hot, you can add more sugar, lime and fish sauce. This jam goes well with so many things - spread it on a sandwich or use it as a dipping sauce. Keep it in the fridge, ready to go. Reheat it gently in a small saucepan over low heat then serve it with your barbecued meats - you'll be blown away by the taste!

Put the sugar and 125 ml (½ cup) water in a large saucepan over medium heat. Cook, stirring, until the sugar dissolves.

Place all the other ingredients in a food processor or blender and blitz on high speed until everything is puréed.

Transfer this mixture to the pan with the sugar and water and stir well. Reduce the heat to low and cook, stirring every 5–10 minutes, until thick, dark and jammy. This will take around 40 minutes.

Before you finish, taste and check for the balance. Fix if necessary then taste again. Transfer to a sterilised sealable jar. The jam will keep for 2–3 weeks.

BRENT'S TIP: When I say check for balance, it's about adjusting the flavours to suit you. If it's too hot, it doesn't mean you can't fix it. Add some more lime juice or tamarind to make it more sour, add more fish sauce to make it saltier, or add more sugar to make it sweeter. Every sauce can be rebalanced to suit your own palate.

THAI GREEN
CURRY PASTE

**MAKES ABOUT 500 G
(2 CUPS)**

8 long green chillies,
 roughly chopped
5 garlic cloves
3 cm piece galangal or ginger,
 roughly chopped
4 eschalots (French shallots),
 roughly chopped
5 kaffir lime leaves, central
 vein removed, roughly
 shredded
25 g (½ cup) chopped
 coriander stems
2 teaspoons shrimp paste
juice and zest of 2 limes
1 lemongrass stem, white part
 only, finely chopped
1 teaspoon coriander seeds
2 tablespoons fish sauce,
 or to taste, or a pinch of salt
pinch of white pepper

Making your own curry paste is easy. I also believe that it can make you a better cook as you learn a lot about balancing flavours, which is so important for cooking in general. Green curry paste is one of my absolute favourites. I often ramp up the lime and ginger and, as I have recently learnt to love chilli, I like to increase the heat too. Play with the ingredients and find out what suits your own palate.

Blitz all the ingredients in a blender or food processor until you have a fine paste. Place in a sterilised sealable jar and keep in the refrigerator for up to 2 weeks.

SMOKED TOMATO RELISH

MAKES ABOUT 560 G (2 CUPS)

1 kg ripe roma tomatoes
40 g (½ cup) smoking sawdust or fine woodchips for smoking
2 red onions, thinly sliced
60 ml (¼ cup) olive oil
2 garlic cloves, crushed
1 teaspoon dried chilli flakes
1 teaspoon coriander seeds
1 tablespoon tomato paste
115 g (½ cup) firmly packed brown sugar
125 ml (½ cup) red wine vinegar

This is really a jazzed-up tomato relish, but the smokiness adds such a depth of flavour. You can use it wherever you'd use normal tomato sauce. You could have it on toast with cheese, use it as a base for pizzas, serve it with barbecued meats, use it as the base of a curry or use it in sandwiches. In this recipe you smoke the tomatoes yourself, but it's not hard. If you love a smoky flavour, this relish is for you!

Using a small knife, cut a shallow cross in the bottom of each tomato. Put the tomatoes in a large bowl and cover with boiling water. Leave for 30 seconds then transfer the tomatoes straight into iced water. Peel the tomatoes and set aside.

Place foil on the bottom of a large wok. Add the smoking sawdust or woodchips and set the wok over high heat, covered. When starting to smoke, add the tomatoes in a steamer basket on a wire rack set 4–5 cm above the smoking mixture, reduce the heat to low, and smoke for 6–8 minutes. Remove and set aside to cool.

While the tomatoes are cooling down, place a large saucepan over medium heat. Cook the onions in the olive oil for 6–8 minutes until soft but not coloured. Add the garlic, chilli flakes and coriander seeds and cook for a further minute. Add the tomato paste and stir over medium heat for 2 minutes. Add the sugar and vinegar.

Cut the cooled tomatoes into quarters, remove the inner membranes and seeds and chop the tomatoes into small chunks. Discard the seeds and membranes. Add the tomatoes to the saucepan and give the mixture a good stir. Bring the mixture to the boil then reduce the heat to medium–low. Cook for 1 hour, stirring occasionally or until thick and gloopy. Taste and adjust the seasoning, then scoop into a sterilised sealable jar and store in the refrigerator for up to 2 weeks.

POACHED APPLES

**MAKES ABOUT 900 G
(4 CUPS)**

1 kg granny smith apples
2 tablespoons brown sugar
375 ml (1½ cups) freshly
    juiced apple juice or good-
    quality apple juice

Using the same principle that when you cook chicken it tastes great cooked in chicken stock, I try to poach fruit in their own juices when possible, as it really boosts the flavour. Poached fruit is great on muesli, in pancakes, or eat it for dessert with ice cream or custard.

Peel, core and cut each apple into 8 pieces.

Place all the ingredients in a medium saucepan over medium–low heat. Cover, bring to the boil and cook for 6–8 minutes, stirring occasionally. You want the apples to be soft but retain their shape.

Scoop the stewed apples and juice into a sterilised sealable jar ready to use any time.

BRENT'S TIP: If you have a juicer, make the juice yourself. You can poach other fruits such as pears, rhubarb and plums. Cook them in their own juice if available, otherwise water will do.

BREA
AND

KFAST
BRUNCH

I worked driving a Bobcat for seven years. Every day I would get up at 4 am. If I didn't have breakfast I wouldn't get a chance to eat for another five hours, so every morning I got up ten minutes early and had a bowl of porridge. But that soon got boring, so I started having muesli – roasting or stewing fruit the day before and incorporating that.

However, weekends have always been special. Breakfast is a leisurely, enjoyable ritual. Every Saturday I get up and make a huge spread. Then my partner, Madison, and I sit at the table reading the paper, dipping crusty bread into our favourite Spanish baked eggs, enjoying the time together. If I don't start the weekend this way, I miss it. A weekend breakfast or brunch is often one of the best opportunities to spend time around the table with loved ones.

I've never been a huge bacon and egg fan – except for after a few beers on a Saturday night! I generally like to take a simple ingredient, like eggs, and add flavours that make it come alive. You don't need to have toast for breakfast. Look at cuisines around the world and see what they have for breakfast – you could even have nasi goreng if you wanted!

In this chapter I've included some of my favourite breakfast and brunch recipes – for quick everyday meals as well as for those times when you'd like something a little indulgent.

MY FAVOURITE BREAKFAST DRINKS

Juices and smoothies are so simple to make. Here are three of my favourite recipes, but you can create your own. Think outside the box and play around with flavours. Get experimenting and see what you love.

BANANA, COCONUT, MANGO AND LIME SMOOTHIE

SERVES 1

1 banana
100 ml coconut milk, chilled
cheeks of 1 mango
juice of 1 lime
dash of natural yoghurt
slice of lime for garnish

This creamy but fresh smoothie is great for breakfast or anytime really. I freeze mango cheeks when they're in season in summer so I have them on hand all year round.

Place all the ingredients in a blender and blitz until smooth. Pour into a glass, garnish with a piece of lime and serve.

BRENT'S TIP: If you want the smoothie to be extra-cold, freeze the fruit beforehand.

CITRUS FRESH

½ pineapple, peeled and
  roughly chopped
1 cm piece of ginger
juice of 3 oranges
juice of 1 lemon
½ bunch mint, leaves torn
1 tablespoon brown sugar

This recipe can be used for a cocktail base too. Add some rum and you have your own twist on a mojito - it's fantastic for guests and parties.

Using a juicer, juice the pineapple and ginger and pour into clean glasses. Add the orange and lemon juice, torn mint leaves and sugar. Stir and serve.

GOING GREEN

SERVES 2

1 bunch mint
70 g (1½ cups) baby English
  spinach, coarse stems
  removed, leaves washed
2 granny smith apples,
  quartered and cored
1 Lebanese cucumber, roughly
  chopped
juice of 1 lemon
2 celery stalks, roughly chopped
½ bunch flat-leaf parsley,
  roughly chopped
3 cm piece ginger, roughly
  chopped
a few ice cubes

This nutritious, fresh drink is bursting with goodness. Start your day with it or drink it before or after a workout.

Push all the ingredients, except the ice, through a juicer. Put the ice cubes in glasses, pour the juice over and serve.

FROM LEFT TO RIGHT: BANANA, COCONUT, MANGO AND LIME SMOOTHIE; CITRUS FRESH; GOING GREEN

SUPER-CRUNCHY, SUPER-HEALTHY MUESLI

**SERVES 2
(OR 1 INCREDIBLY
HUNGRY PERSON)**

30 g (¼ cup) slivered almonds
2 figs
2 fresh medjool dates
1 apple, cored
65 g (½ cup) plain oven-
   toasted muesli
30 g (¼ cup) pepitas
   (pumpkin seeds)
30 g (¼ cup) raisins
250 g (1 cup) natural Greek-
   style yoghurt
2 tablespoons honey
30 g (¼ cup) fresh
   pomegranate seeds
35 g (¼ cup) chopped
   pistachio nuts

There are so many exciting flavours in this muesli that you'll enjoy it to the last bite! I love fresh pomegranate – the more I have, the more I use! It adds such a fresh pop of tangy flavour. The medjool dates add a delish sweetness to the dish.

Dry-fry the almonds in a frying pan over medium heat for 5 minutes, or until lightly toasted. Set aside and allow to cool.

Cut the figs into wedges and the dates and apple into pieces. Combine in a bowl with the muesli, pepitas, almonds and raisins, then stir in the yoghurt and honey.

Serve topped with the pomegranate seeds and pistachio nuts.

BRENT'S TIP: If you're feeling game, you could add a few drops of rosewater. It goes well with the flavours but be careful – it's super-strong!

FOOLPROOF FLUFFY PANCAKES

SERVES 4 (MAKES 12 PANCAKES)

PANCAKES
300 g (2 cups) self-raising flour
2 teaspoons caster sugar
2 eggs, lightly beaten
375 ml (1½ cups) milk
60 g butter, plus 1 tablespoon melted butter

Why buy pancake mix when it's so easy to make your own? You can't really go wrong with these American-style pancakes. I've suggested some toppings (opposite) but you can create your own - think of crunchy nuts, hot stewed fruits and sweet syrups, or even just sugar and citrus fruit. Kids will love getting involved and helping you to top them.

For the pancakes, sift the flour and sugar into a mixing bowl. Make a well in the centre and pour in the eggs, milk and the 1 tablespoon of melted butter. Whisk to combine the ingredients. (Don't be alarmed if there are a few little lumps, as it doesn't matter.)

In a large frying pan over medium heat, melt about a teaspoon of the butter until foaming. Working in batches, pour about 60 ml (¼ cup) batter into the pan at a time – it should spread out to be around 10–12 cm in diameter. Cook the pancake until bubbles form and pop on the top, about 2–3 minutes. Flip the pancake over and cook the other side for another minute or two.

Remove the pancake from the pan and transfer it to a warm plate (or store in an oven heated to low), while you cook the remaining pancakes.

Wipe the pan with paper towel and repeat with the remaining butter and batter, until all the pancakes are cooked.

Serve a stack of 3 pancakes for each person with the topping of your choice (see opposite).

TOPPING IDEAS

APPLE AND MASCARPONE TOPPING

100 g mascarpone
pinch of ground cinnamon
1 teaspoon icing sugar
225 g (1 cup) Poached apples
(page 33)
maple syrup for drizzling
pistachio nuts for sprinkling
(optional)

Whisk together the mascarpone, cinnamon and icing sugar.

Warm the apples in a small saucepan over low heat or in a microwave on Medium for 2 minutes, stirring halfway through cooking time.

Serve the pancakes with a dollop of the mascarpone mixture and some of the warmed apples, then drizzle with maple syrup and sprinkle over the pistachio nuts, if using.

BANANA, PEANUT AND CHOCOLATE TOPPING

2 tablespoons peanut butter
1 tablespoon brown sugar
2 bananas, peeled and halved
lengthways
small handful dark chocolate
chips for sprinkling

Preheat a grill to medium–high.

In a small heatproof bowl over a small saucepan of simmering water, gently melt the peanut butter, or heat it in a microwave on Low in 15 second bursts until it has melted.

Sprinkle the sugar on the cut side of the bananas and cook them under the grill until the sugar has started to caramelise, about 3–5 minutes.

Serve the bananas on top of the pancakes, drizzle with the melted peanut butter and sprinkle with the chocolate chips.

CHOCOLATE–HAZELNUT AND STRAWBERRY TOPPING

heaps of chocolate–hazelnut
spread
fresh strawberries
icing sugar for dusting

Heat the chocolate–hazelnut spread gently in a microwave on Low in 15 second bursts until it has melted. Spread it liberally over the pancakes and top with fresh strawberries. Dust with icing sugar to finish.

SPICY MEXICAN BEAN WRAPS
WITH CORN SALSA

SERVES 4

8 large (about 20 cm in diameter) wraps or store-bought or homemade tortillas (see page 25)
chopped coriander leaves to serve
sour cream to serve

MEXICAN BEANS
1 tablespoon olive oil
1 onion, thinly sliced
2 garlic cloves, crushed
1 teaspoon ground cumin
$\frac{1}{2}$ teaspoon cayenne pepper
1 red capsicum, thinly sliced
400 g tinned diced tomatoes
400 g tinned cannellini or butter beans, drained and rinsed

Wraps are a super-simple dish that kids can get involved with, helping to fill them with the various ingredients. You can play around with the flavours if you like. I always tend to add a bit more lime juice and coriander as I love them!

Heat the olive oil in a frying pan over medium heat. Add the onion and garlic and sauté for 2–3 minutes, but don't allow them to colour. Add the spices and stir until well combined. Add the capsicum and sauté for a further 2–3 minutes. Pour in the tomatoes, reduce the heat to low and let the mixture reduce for 4–5 minutes. Add the beans and stir to combine. Taste for seasoning. If the sauce is getting over-reduced, just add a little water or remove the pan from the heat. It should be thick and gluggy but still ooze. Let the mixture bubble away over a very low heat for a further 2–3 minutes while you make the salsa.

CORN SALSA

1 tomato
1 avocado
1 eschalot (French shallot)
1 jalapeño
small handful coriander
  leaves, chopped
310 g tinned corn kernels,
  drained and rinsed
juice of 1 lime
dash of olive oil

For the corn salsa, chop the tomato, avocado, eschalot and jalapeño to roughly the same size as the corn kernels. Transfer to a bowl with the coriander, corn, lime juice and olive oil and toss to combine. Season and taste – the salsa should be tangy and full of flavour. Play with the flavours until you get the balance right – but remember to only add a tiny bit of an ingredient at a time!

Just before you're ready to serve, heat the wraps according to the packet directions. Spoon the bean mixture into the centre of the wraps, top with the salsa and finish with a little fresh coriander and sour cream. Roll up the wraps and serve. Delish!

SPANISH BAKED EGGS

SERVES 2

250 g chorizo, sliced
2 eschalots (French shallots),
    thinly sliced
1 garlic clove, finely chopped
¼ teaspoon smoked paprika
¼ teaspoon ground cumin
¼ teaspoon cayenne pepper
2 tablespoons sherry vinegar
    or red wine vinegar
400 g tinned diced tomatoes
1 teaspoon baby capers,
    rinsed (optional)
2 anchovy fillets, chopped
    (optional)
2 eggs, at room temperature
chopped flat-leaf parsley for
    garnish
chargrilled or toasted bread
    to serve

I'm a big fan of Spanish food, especially the smoky paprika and chorizo, and this is one of my favourite breakfasts. Remember that the capers and anchovies are very salty, so taste, taste, taste throughout cooking to check the seasoning.

Preheat the oven to 190°C (or 170°C for a fan-forced oven).

Cook the chorizo in a small ovenproof frying pan over medium heat until the oil is released and the chorizo is caramelised, about 2–3 minutes. Add the eschalots and garlic and sauté for a further 2 minutes. Add the paprika, cumin and cayenne pepper and sauté for a further minute or until fragrant.

Add the vinegar and deglaze the pan, cooking until the liquid has almost evaporated, about 2 minutes. Add the tomatoes, capers (if using) and anchovies (if using), stir well to combine and continue to cook for another minute.

If you want to serve the eggs in individual dishes, transfer the mixture to two 300 ml ovenproof dishes, otherwise you can just leave the mixture in the frying pan. Make a small indentation in the mixture in the pan or each dish, and break an egg into it. Bake in the oven for 8–10 minutes, depending on how runny you want your yolk.

Top with some freshly chopped parsley before serving with the chargrilled or toasted bread.

BRENT'S TIP: If you're in a hurry, you can put your baking dishes in the oven at preheating stage to warm them up. This will speed up the cooking of the eggs – but remember the dishes will be smoking hot!

MY ULTIMATE HANGOVER BREKKY

SERVES 2

2 pork and fennel sausages

4 rashers bacon

150 g black pudding, thickly
 sliced

30 g butter

3 thyme sprigs

80 g Swiss brown mushrooms,
 quartered

4 baby onions, halved,
 outer skin and one extra
 layer removed

60 ml (¼ cup) olive oil

80 ml (⅓ cup) balsamic
 vinegar

4 eggs

4 slices sourdough bread

I don't often have a huge breakfast, but when I do this is the one. It's quite indulgent, but absolutely delicious - and ideal if you've had a big night out! I like to serve this with my Smoked tomato relish (page 32).

Preheat the oven to 200°C (or 180°C for a fan-forced oven).

In a large frying pan over medium heat, cook the sausages for 5 minutes. Tip any excess fat out of the pan and then add the bacon. Cook until the bacon has released some of its fat and then add the black pudding and cook until lightly caramelised, about 2 minutes. Transfer all the ingredients to paper towel to absorb any remaining fat. Cover with foil and keep warm.

Meanwhile, heat the butter in a small ovenproof frying pan over medium–low heat until foaming. Add the thyme sprigs and mushrooms and sauté for 2–3 minutes, basting the mushrooms with the butter. Remove the mushrooms, set aside and keep warm.

Wipe the frying pan clean with paper towel.

Place the onions, cut side down, in the pan and cook in 1 tablespoon of the olive oil until just starting to caramelise, about 3 minutes. Transfer the pan to the oven and roast the onion for 8–10 minutes.

Remove the pan from the oven and place it back over medium heat. Add the balsamic vinegar and cook for 2–3 minutes until the liquid reduces.

Heat the remaining oil in a separate frying pan over medium heat. Once hot, break the eggs into the pan and baste them with the oil until they are cooked sunny-side up.

Toast the sourdough bread, preferably in a ridged pan so you have nice griddle marks on both sides.

Transfer the eggs to serving plates, along with the sausages, bacon, black pudding, mushrooms, onions and toasted bread.

VARIATIONS

For an equally awesome vegetarian option, substitute the bacon, sausage and black pudding with haloumi cheese, English spinach and my Mexican beans (see page 48). Simply pan-fry the haloumi for 30 seconds on each side and sauté the spinach in a little butter for 2 minutes.

CHURROS

250 ml (1 cup) water
100 g unsalted butter, chopped
150 g (1 cup) plain flour
pinch of salt
3 eggs
vegetable oil for deep-frying
40 g (1/3 cup) icing sugar
2 tablespoons ground cinnamon

DIPPING SAUCE
125 ml (1/2 cup) milk
250 g dark chocolate (at least 70% cocoa solids), roughly chopped

These are great any time, but I like them for breakfast when I'm feeling indulgent. I sometimes eat them with caramel sauce (see page 199) instead of the chocolate dipping sauce.

Put the water and butter in a medium saucepan over high heat and bring to the boil, stirring until the butter melts. Remove the pan from the heat and add the flour and salt, stirring constantly with a wooden spoon until the dough forms a ball and is no longer sticking to the side of the pan. Keep stirring the dough to release as much steam as possible in order to cool it down. The dough should be quite stiff but you should still be able to pipe it. If it's too stiff, add a little extra water. When the dough is cool, add the eggs one at a time, mixing well with a wooden spoon, ensuring each egg is fully incorporated before adding the next. Put the dough in a large piping bag with a 1.5 cm star nozzle.

For the dipping sauce, heat the milk and chocolate in a small saucepan over low heat, stirring continuously until the chocolate has melted and is well combined with the milk. Set aside but keep warm.

Fill a medium saucepan over medium–high heat one-third full with the vegetable oil, or turn a deep-fryer to 180°C.

Check your oil is hot enough by putting a wooden spoon handle in the oil. It's hot enough if the oil bubbles around the handle. Working in batches, pipe your dough straight into the oil and use a pair of scissors to snip it off at your desired length – about 8 cm is good. Fry the churros for 6–7 minutes or until they are a deep golden colour and cooked through. Scoop them out with a slotted spoon and immediately transfer to paper towel. Mix the icing sugar and cinnamon together and dust the churros. Serve with the dipping sauce.

FRENCH TOAST
WITH BAKED RHUBARB, ALMONDS AND VANILLA ICE CREAM

SERVES 4

30 g (⅓ cup) flaked almonds (optional)
1 bunch rhubarb, cut into 5 cm lengths
juice and zest of 2 oranges, plus extra zest to serve
55 g (¼ cup) caster sugar
6 eggs
125 ml (½ cup) pouring cream
8 thickly cut slices brioche loaf
60 g butter
vanilla ice cream to serve

Using brioche instead of white bread adds even more sweetness to this French toast. The almonds can be replaced with any nuts, and other poached fruit, such as apples or pears, can be used instead of the rhubarb.

Preheat the oven to 220°C (or 200°C for a fan-forced oven).

Dry-fry the almonds (if using) in a frying pan over medium heat for 5 minutes, or until lightly toasted. Allow to cool.

In a baking tray, combine the rhubarb and orange juice and zest then sprinkle with the sugar. Cover with foil and bake in the oven for 10–12 minutes or until tender. Set aside in the tray.

In a mixing bowl, lightly whisk together the eggs and cream. Dip the slices of brioche in the egg and cream mixture, turning the pieces to coat and soaking them in the mixture for 1–2 minutes.

Put half the butter in a large non-stick frying pan over medium heat. When the butter starts to foam, add half the brioche slices and fry for about 2 minutes on each side. Once cooked, transfer the French toast to paper towel to drain. Repeat with the remaining butter and brioche slices.

To serve, top the French toast with some rhubarb mixture, vanilla ice cream, a sprinkling of toasted almonds (if using) and top with the extra orange zest. Drizzle with any left-over rhubarb syrup from the pan.

BRENT'S TIP: Check the rhubarb after it has been cooking for 10 minutes – you want it soft and tender, but you don't want it to start falling apart and becoming fibrous.

SNACKS AND LUNCH

I look forward to food – to making it and eating it. It should always be a joy, not a chore, so why not spend that little bit of extra time the night before to prepare something that tastes good for lunch, rather than eating the same thing day in, day out? Sometimes it's not even about time, it's about thinking creatively. Don't throw your leftovers away – use them for lunch the next day. Left-over meats and vegetables make great sandwich fillings, or are great on top of baked potatoes.

Many of the recipes in this chapter you can take to work with you – especially if you have a microwave or a sandwich press on hand. Instead of buying a sandwich, take a quesadilla to work and warm it up in a sandwich press. It's better than anything you could buy at a sandwich shop!

This chapter also includes a range of tasty snacks, from simple dips made with unusual flavours and textures, to crunchy cheese-filled potato balls and potato wedges with creamy blue cheese sauce. Why buy potato chips when you can easily make snacks this good!

THREE EASY DIPS

Dips are so damn easy to put together. Here are three easy and tasty recipes, but see page 14 for some guidelines on making your own creations. Serve the dips with toasted slices of Italian bread, breadsticks, baby vegetables, vegetables cut into batons or even toasted pitta bread wedges.

BEETROOT AND GOAT'S CHEESE DIP

MAKES ABOUT 300 G (1¼ CUPS)

2 medium (350 g in total) beetroot, peeled and sliced
2 tablespoons balsamic vinegar
60 g (¼ cup) natural Greek-style yoghurt
100 g goat's cheese, crumbled
leaves from 1 thyme sprig
olive oil to drizzle

Steam the beetroot over a large saucepan of boiling water for 15–20 minutes or until tender.

Put the balsamic vinegar in a small frying pan over medium heat and cook for about 2–3 minutes until reduced by half. When syrupy, add the beetroot and toss to coat.

Transfer the beetroot to a food processor or blender, or use a hand-held blender, and blitz until smooth. Add the yoghurt and blitz again. Add 90 g of the crumbled goat's cheese and fold it through. Season with salt and pepper.

Transfer the dip to a serving bowl and top with the remaining goat's cheese, thyme leaves and a drizzle of olive oil.

BRENT'S TIPS: You can replace the fresh beetroot with 425 g tinned sliced beetroot, well drained. Wear disposable gloves if you're worried about staining your hands when preparing the beetroot.

SARDINE DIP

MAKES ABOUT 125 G (½ CUP)

105 g tinned sardines in oil,
    oil reserved
1 garlic clove, finely chopped
1 eschalot (French shallot),
    finely chopped
2 tablespoons natural Greek-
    style yoghurt
1 teaspoon lemon juice
finely chopped flat-leaf
    parsley to serve

Put the reserved sardine oil in a small frying pan over medium heat. Add the garlic and eschalot and sweat for 2–3 minutes, stirring occasionally. Add the sardines and remove from the heat.

Transfer the sardine mixture to a food processor or blender, or use a hand-held blender, and blitz until smooth. Add the yoghurt and lemon juice and pulse again.

Transfer to a serving bowl and top with the parsley.

BUTTER BEAN AND PISTACHIO DIP

MAKES ABOUT 250 G
(1 CUP)

1 garlic clove, crushed
1 eschalot (French shallot),
    finely chopped
1 teaspoon olive oil
½ teaspoon ground cumin
½ teaspoon sweet paprika,
    plus extra to serve
¼ teaspoon chilli powder
400 g tinned butter beans,
    drained and rinsed
juice of ½ lemon
35 g (¼ cup) pistachio nuts,
    plus extra to serve
coriander leaves to serve

In a small frying pan over medium heat, sweat the garlic and eschalot in the olive oil for 2–3 minutes. Add the cumin, paprika, chilli powder and a dash of water and cook for a further minute, until fragrant.

Transfer to a small food processor or blender, add the butter beans and blitz until smooth, or use a hand-held blender. Add the lemon juice and pulse again. Transfer to a serving bowl.

Lightly toast the pistachio nuts in a dry frying pan until golden, about 5 minutes. Allow to cool then lightly crush them using a mortar and pestle. Fold the crushed nuts through the dip. Serve with a dusting of paprika, a few pistachio nuts and the coriander.

BRENT'S TIP: Add a dash of water to keep the mixture moving in your blender, if required.

FROM LEFT TO RIGHT:
BUTTER BEAN AND
PISTACHIO DIP; SARDINE
DIP; BEETROOT AND
GOAT'S CHEESE DIP

WEDGES
WITH BLUE CHEESE SAUCE

SERVES 4–6

5 desiree potatoes (about
   1 kg in total), unpeeled
2 tablespoons duck fat,
   melted
salt flakes
1 teaspoon cayenne pepper
lemon wedges to serve

BLUE CHEESE SAUCE
20 g butter
½ garlic clove, crushed
2 teaspoons plain flour
150 ml milk
125 g blue cheese (I like King
   Island Roaring Forties),
   crumbled

These wedges with a creamy blue cheese sauce are indulgent but delish! Don't be shy with the lemon as the acidity really cuts through the richness of the dipping sauce.

For the wedges, preheat the oven to 220°C (or 200°C for a fan-forced oven). Line 2 baking trays with baking paper.

Cut the potatoes in half then into thick wedges and place them on the lined baking trays. Drizzle with the duck fat, season with the salt flakes and cayenne pepper and turn the wedges to coat.

Roast the wedges for 35–40 minutes, shaking the trays a couple of times during cooking, until they are golden and crispy.

To make the dipping sauce, melt the butter in a small saucepan over low heat. Add the garlic and let it sweat for 2 minutes. Add the flour and cook, stirring continuously, for a further 2 minutes, but don't let the mixture colour. Whisk in the milk – the mixture will start to thicken pretty quickly, so whisk continuously to remove any lumps, about 2–3 minutes.

Add the blue cheese, in batches, waiting for each clump to melt before adding the next. Remove the sauce from the heat and serve while still warm and melted, with the potato wedges. Serve the lemon wedges on the side.

EGGPLANT CHIPS
WITH SPICY KEWPIE MAYO

vegetable oil for deep-frying
1 large (about 500 g) eggplant
60 g (¼ cup) salt
3 eggs
150 g (1 cup) plain flour
120 g (2 cups) panko crumbs
salt flakes

SPICY KEWPIE MAYO
125 g (½ cup) kewpie
   mayonnaise
60 ml (¼ cup) sriracha hot
   chilli sauce

These eggplant chips are crispy on the outside and creamy on the inside. I use kewpie mayo as it's a bit more acidic than regular mayonnaise. I've spiced it up with a little sriracha hot chilli sauce, which is a Thai-style fermented chilli sauce that's actually made in the United States.

Fill a large saucepan two-thirds full with vegetable oil and then turn the heat to medium to let the oil heat up.

Slice the eggplant in half lengthways, then in half widthways, and then cut it into small wedges. Place in a colander and sprinkle with the salt. Leave for 10 minutes to expel any excess liquid. Brush the eggplant clean and transfer to paper towel to absorb any liquid and excess salt.

Crack the eggs into a medium bowl and lightly whisk them. Put the flour in a second bowl and the panko crumbs in a third bowl. Dip each eggplant chip first in the flour, then the egg, then the panko crumbs. Dip back in the egg and panko crumbs again for a thicker coating.

Check the oil temperature by placing a wooden spoon handle in the oil. If the oil bubbles around the handle (or the temperature reads 180°C on a thermometer), the oil is hot enough. Place batches of the eggplant chips in the oil and fry for 4–5 minutes or until dark golden brown and crispy. Transfer straight to paper towel to absorb any excess oil and season with salt flakes. Repeat with the remaining eggplant chips.

For the spicy kewpie mayo, mix the kewpie mayonnaise and sriracha in a small bowl. Serve with the eggplant chips.

GOOEY, CHEESY POTATO BALLS

600 g potatoes, peeled and
quartered
20 g unsalted butter
2 eschalots (French shallots),
finely diced
1 garlic clove, crushed
35 g (¼ cup) plain flour
2 eggs, lightly beaten
90 g (1½ cups) panko crumbs
75 g (½ cup) grated
mozzarella
60 g (½ cup) grated smoked
cheddar
vegetable oil for deep-frying
lemon wedges to serve
Chipotle mayo (page 23)
to serve

You can eat these crispy potato balls on their own, served with the lemon wedges and mayo, but I think they'd also be awesome with the Potato and leek soup with bacon and chives (page 126).

Put the potatoes in a medium saucepan over high heat, cover with cold water and season with salt. Bring to the boil, then reduce the heat to low and simmer for 15–20 minutes or until tender. Drain the potatoes and mash until smooth. Set aside to cool. (You will need about 460 g/2 cups of mash for this recipe.)

Put the butter in a small frying pan over medium heat. When foaming, add the eschalots and garlic and sweat for 2–3 minutes. Remove the pan from the heat to cool down for 5 minutes.

Put the flour, egg and panko crumbs in 3 separate bowls.

In a large bowl, using clean hands, combine the mashed potato, the eschalot and garlic mixture and the grated mozzarella and cheddar. Season to taste.

Roll the mixture into balls the size of ping-pong balls. Dip the balls first in the flour, then the egg and finish in the panko crumbs, ensuring a thick coating. (You can double-dip back into the egg and panko crumbs for a thicker coating.)

Fill a medium saucepan one-third full with vegetable oil and set it over medium heat. (Or heat a deep-fryer to 180°C.) Check that the oil is hot enough by dipping a wooden spoon handle in it. If the oil bubbles around the handle, then it's hot enough.

Using a slotted spoon carefully drop the balls in the oil – treat them gently so they don't fall apart – and cook until golden brown, about 5–6 minutes. When they are cooked, transfer the balls to paper towel to absorb any excess oil and season with salt. Serve hot with the lemon wedges and chipotle mayo on the side.

ROASTED JACKET SPUDS

SERVES 4

4 large (1.2 kg in total)
   potatoes
1 teaspoon salt flakes

I grew up eating baked potatoes and I still love them. I often have these for lunch at home, or take them to work if I have a microwave handy. I also like to wrap them in foil and chuck them in the coals of the barbecue.

Preheat the oven to 220°C (or 200°C for a fan-forced oven).

Wash and scrub the potatoes to remove any grit, then allow them to dry and dust with salt.

Wrap the potatoes in foil and bake them for 1 hour or until tender.

Remove the potatoes from the oven and open the foil parcel. Cut three-quarters of the way through the potatoes and open them out. Fill with your desired topping (see opposite and on pages 76–77).

TOPPINGS

MEXICAN NACHOS

250 g (1 cup) Mexican beans (see page 48)
1 avocado, thinly sliced
125 g tinned corn kernels, drained and rinsed
large handful corn chips, lightly crushed
125 g (1 cup) grated tasty cheese
60 g (¼ cup) sour cream

Warm the beans in a small saucepan over medium–low heat for 4–5 minutes. Top the potatoes with the avocado, followed by the beans and corn. Scatter over the corn chips and cheese and finish with a dollop of sour cream.

BACON, SOUR CREAM AND CHIVES

4 rashers bacon, thinly sliced
80 g sour cream
8 chives, thinly sliced

Pan-fry the bacon until crisp and golden, then drain on paper towel. Scatter the bacon over the potatoes. Finish with a dollop of sour cream and scatter over the chives.

CHILLI CON CARNE

250 g (1 cup) Chilli con carne (page 147)
90 g (⅔ cup) grated tasty cheese

Warm the chilli con carne in a small saucepan over medium–low heat for 4–5 minutes. Fill the potatoes with the warmed chilli con carne and top with the cheese.

>

ROASTED JACKET SPUDS
WITH MEXICAN NACHOS
TOPPING

continued from page 73

MORE TOPPINGS FOR ROASTED JACKET SPUDS

KIMCHI AND SHREDDED CHICKEN

175 g (1 cup) shredded poached or left-over roast or barbecued chicken
250 g (1 cup) Kimchi (page 26)
kewpie or Quick whole egg mayo (page 23) to serve

Warm the chicken in a frying pan over medium heat for about 1–2 minutes. Fill the potatoes with kimchi, top with the chicken and drizzle with mayo.

TUNA MAYO WITH PICKLED ESCHALOTS

180 g tinned tuna chunks in olive oil, drained
2 tablespoons Quick whole egg mayo (page 23)
Pickled eschalots (see page 134) to serve

Combine the tuna and mayo in a small bowl and season to taste. Fill the potatoes with the tuna mixture and scatter over the pickled eschalots.

CURRIED EGG WITH ROCKET OR WATERCRESS

large handful watercress sprigs or wild rocket leaves, washed
1 quantity Curried egg (see page 80)

Fill the potatoes with watercress or rocket and top with the curried egg. Season to taste.

HERBED MUSHROOMS WITH GARLIC AND SOUR CREAM

20 g butter
200 g Swiss brown or button
    mushrooms, sliced
1 thyme sprig
1 garlic clove, crushed
2 tablespoons sour cream

Melt the butter in a medium frying pan over medium heat until foaming. Add the mushrooms, thyme sprig and garlic and cook, stirring occasionally, until the mushrooms are tender and lightly browned, about 5–6 minutes. Stir in the sour cream and season to taste. Fill the potatoes with the mushroom mixture.

SALMON WITH MISO BUTTER AND SESAME SEEDS

1 tablespoon sesame seeds
1 teaspoon olive oil
200 g salmon fillet
60 g unsalted butter, softened
2 teaspoons white miso paste

Heat a small frying pan over medium–high heat. Dry-fry the sesame seeds for 3–4 minutes or until lightly toasted. Set aside. Add the oil to the same frying pan, add the salmon and cook for 2–3 minutes each side until done to your liking. Set aside to rest for 5 minutes. Whisk the butter until smooth, then add the miso and whisk until well combined. Flake the salmon and top the potatoes with it. Add a dollop of miso butter and a sprinkle of toasted sesame seeds.

SUPER-SIMPLE
SANGAS

There are bakeries out there filled with huge selections of bread. If you love sandwiches, why not try a different type of bread every day? Use leftovers for fillings and pair them with bold flavours. Experiment! I've provided a few ideas below and on pages 80–81.

SERVES 4

PORK AND KIMCHI ROLLS

125 ml (½ cup) rice wine vinegar
2 tablespoons caster sugar
2 Lebanese cucumbers, thinly sliced
left-over pork belly (see page 180)
1 teaspoon sesame oil
kewpie mayonnaise to serve
1 baguette (about 300 g)
260 g (1 cup) Kimchi (page 26)
handful coriander leaves
3 spring onions, thinly sliced
1 large carrot, julienned
1 tablespoon toasted sesame seeds

In a small saucepan put 125 ml (½ cup) water, the rice wine vinegar and sugar. Bring to the boil then add the sliced cucumber. Turn off the heat and leave the cucumber to cool down and pickle in the liquid, about 30 minutes.

Slice the pork belly into 1 cm thick slices. Reheat it in a frying pan with the sesame oil.

To assemble, drain the pickled cucumber and pat it dry. Spread a layer of kewpie mayo on the base of the baguette, then top with the pickled cucumber, pork belly, a layer of kimchi, the coriander, spring onion, julienned carrot and finally a sprinkle of sesame seeds. Slice the baguette into 4 and serve.

For picnics or snacks, slice the baguette into 5 cm thick pieces and you have yourself 8 individual rolls.

continued from page 78

WHOLEMEAL CURRIED EGG AND CRESS SANGA

8 slices wholemeal bread
butter, softened, for
    spreading
1 baby cos lettuce, leaves
    separated
handful watercress

CURRIED EGG
8 large eggs
60 g (¼ cup) Parsley mayo
    (page 23)
1 teaspoon dijon mustard
1 teaspoon curry powder

To make the curried egg, put the eggs in a medium saucepan and cover with cold water. Bring to the boil over medium–high heat and boil for 4 minutes. Drain the eggs and run them under cold water to cool rapidly, then peel.

Put the eggs in a medium bowl and mash them with a fork. Add the mayonnaise, mustard and curry powder and mix until everything is well combined. Season with salt and pepper.

Spread the bread with butter and top all 8 slices with curried egg. Add lettuce and watercress to half of the bread slices, then close the sandwiches with the remaining bread slices.

TOASTED CHICKEN AND EGG FOCACCIA WITH MUSTARD

4 focaccia rolls
butter, softened, for
    spreading
90 g (⅓ cup) dijon mustard
4 hard-boiled eggs, sliced
2 poached chicken breasts
    (see page 15), shredded
1 small red onion, thinly sliced
1 avocado, thinly sliced

Slice the focaccia in half and toast the cut side under a hot grill. Remove the focaccia from the grill and assemble the sandwich.

Butter the toasted side of each piece of focaccia. Spread the 4 bases with mustard, then top with sliced egg, shredded chicken, onion and avocado. Season with salt and pepper. Close the rolls with the top slices of focaccia.

SMOKED CHEDDAR TOASTIE

butter, softened, for
   spreading
8 x 2 cm thick sourdough
   bread slices
190 g (²/₃ cup) Smoked tomato
   relish (page 32)
24 slices jamón ibérico
   (Spanish cured ham)
200 g smoked cheddar
   cheese, grated

Heat a sandwich press or a large heavy-based frying pan over
medium heat.

Butter one side of each slice of bread. Top the unbuttered side
of 4 slices of bread with the relish, jamón and cheese. Close the
sandwich with the remaining bread slice, buttered-side out. Toast
the sandwich in a sandwich press (or frying pan, cooking both sides)
until the outside is golden and the cheese is oozing and gooey.

LEFT-OVER ROAST VEG FOCACCIA WITH SMOKED CHEDDAR AND ROAST BEEF

4 focaccia rolls
190 g (²/₃ cup) Smoked tomato
   relish (page 32)
large handful baby English
   spinach leaves
8 slices left-over or deli-
   bought roast beef
2–3 cups left-over roast
   potato, pumpkin, sweet
   potato, carrot, onion or
   even garlic
200 g smoked cheddar
   cheese, grated

Heat a sandwich press or a large heavy-based frying pan over
medium heat.

Slice the focaccia rolls in half and spread the base with the tomato
relish, then top with the spinach, beef, roasted veggies and cheese.
Close the focaccia with the remaining slices. Toast the sandwich in a
sandwich press (or frying pan, cooking both sides) until the outside
is golden and the cheese is oozing and gooey.

EGG CRÊPES
WITH CHAR SIU PORK

SERVES 4

240 g pork fillet
2 tablespoons char siu pork
   marinade
1 teaspoon peanut oil
1 tablespoon sesame oil
8 eggs
200 g (2²/₃ cups) finely
   shredded Chinese cabbage
   (wombok)
2 tablespoons soy sauce
1 teaspoon honey
90 g (1 cup) bean sprouts
4 spring onions, thinly sliced
sriracha hot chilli sauce
   to serve
2 teaspoons toasted sesame
   seeds

This dish sounds complex but if you marinate the pork the night before, it's only a 30-minute meal.

Combine the pork and char siu marinade in a small bowl and set aside to marinate for at least 1 hour.

Preheat the oven to 200°C (or 180°C for a fan-forced oven). Put the peanut oil in a large ovenproof frying pan over high heat. Season the pork with salt and pepper then sear it in the pan on all sides until lightly golden, about 2–3 minutes. Transfer the frying pan to the oven and roast the pork for 12–15 minutes. Remove from the oven and transfer to a plate. Lightly cover with foil and allow the meat to rest for 10 minutes.

Meanwhile, heat a large wok over high heat. Add a few drops of the sesame oil and, using paper towel, wipe the oil around the wok being careful not to burn yourself. Heat the oil until smoking.

Lightly whisk the eggs in a jug, then pour a quarter of the egg mixture at a time into the wok. Immediately grab the handle of the wok and swirl the egg around the inside of the wok as high up the sides as you can go, so the wok has an even coating of egg. Cook for a further minute until the edges start to lift and the top is set, then remove the egg crêpe with your fingers or with the help of a spatula, being careful not to burn yourself. Repeat the process to get 4 crêpes, adding a few more drops of sesame oil before you cook each one. Transfer the crêpes to a warm plate and cover with a clean tea towel. Keep the wok on the heat and add the remaining sesame oil. Add the cabbage and stir-fry it for 1 minute. Add the soy sauce and honey and stir-fry for a further minute, until just wilted. Transfer the cabbage to a warm plate.

To assemble, slice the pork into 1 cm slices. Lay the crêpes flat on a work surface and top with the cabbage mixture, bean sprouts, spring onion, sliced pork and a little sriracha. Sprinkle with sesame seeds. Fold the crêpe over to enclose the filling. Serve with some extra sriracha sauce.

CHICKEN RICE PAPER ROLLS
WITH DIPPING SAUCE

SERVES 4 (MAKES 12)

50 g rice vermicelli noodles

1 Lebanese cucumber, halved
  lengthways

12 large (22 cm) round rice
  paper wrappers (banh
  trang)

175 g (1 cup) shredded
  poached chicken or left-over
  barbecued chicken

60 g (1 cup) coarsely shredded
  iceberg lettuce

1 carrot, peeled and julienned

large handful coriander leaves

12 Vietnamese mint leaves

DIPPING SAUCE

30 ml fish sauce

1 tablespoon lime juice

1 tablespoon rice wine
  vinegar

1 tablespoon finely chopped
  roasted peanuts

2 teaspoons shaved palm
  sugar

1 long red chilli, finely
  chopped

½ garlic clove, crushed

2 tablespoons water

Classic salad items and noodles make a great base for rice paper rolls. Try swapping the chicken for marinated char siu pork fillet (see page 82), Chinese barbecued duck, deep-fried firm tofu strips or cooked prawns.

For the dipping sauce, combine all the ingredients in a small bowl and stir until the sugar dissolves. Set side.

Place the noodles in a medium heatproof bowl and cover with warm water. Soak for 10 minutes or until tender, then drain well.

Scoop the seeds out of the cucumber with a small spoon and cut the cucumber into 12 batons.

Making one roll at a time, immerse a rice paper wrapper in a bowl of warm water, then drain immediately. Top the bottom third of the wrapper with a bundle of the noodles and a drizzle of the dipping sauce, then add some chicken, a few strips of lettuce, a strip of cucumber and some carrot, making sure the pile is neat. Top with some herbs and then turn up the bottom of the wrapper to cover the filling. Carefully turn both sides of the wraper in on top of the first fold and roll up gently to enclose the filling. Repeat with the remaining wrappers and filling.

Serve with the remaining dipping sauce.

CHICKEN AND CHEESE
QUESADILLAS

SERVES 4 (OR 2 VERY
HUNGRY PEOPLE)

olive oil spray
4 large (23 cm) tortillas,
   store-bought or homemade
   (see page 25)
95 g (⅓ cup) Smoked tomato
   relish (page 32)
350 g (2 cups) shredded
   poached chicken or left-over
   barbecued chicken
125 g (1 cup) grated smoked
   cheddar cheese
handful baby English spinach
   leaves
120 g (about 10) bocconcini
   balls
lemon or lime wedges
   to garnish

I've only started making these recently, but they are just the best and I eat them all the time now. I love the textural and flavour contrasts – the crunchy fried tortilla, the gooey cheese, the smoky relish and the fresh lime.

Heat a large frying pan over medium heat and lightly spray it with olive oil.

Lay 2 tortillas flat on a work surface. Spread the tortillas with relish then top with chicken, half of the grated cheese and the spinach. Tear the bocconcini balls in half and dot them around the tortillas, then add the remaining grated cheese. Top both with a second tortilla. Place one quesadilla in the frying pan and cook until golden on one side, 2–3 minutes.

Slide the quesadilla out onto a plate and, moving quickly, flip it over and slide it back into the pan. Cook until the second side is golden and the cheese has melted. Remove the quesadilla from the pan and cut it into quarters. Repeat with the remaining quesadilla then serve with the lemon or lime wedges.

VARIATION

For a bean, corn and jalapeño quesadilla, heat a large frying pan over medium heat and lightly spray it with olive oil. Lay 2 tortillas flat on a work surface. Top the tortillas with 250 g (1 cup) Mexican beans (see page 48), 125 g tinned corn kernels, 60 g (½ cup) grated tasty cheese, 60 g (⅓ cup) pickled jalapeños and 4 thinly sliced spring onions. Top with another 60 g (½ cup) grated tasty cheese and a second tortilla. Follow the cooking instructions above.

CHICKEN AND CHEESE
QUESADILLAS

BARBEC AND SALADS

UES

The smell of a barbecue brings back memories. It reminds me of great experiences, of holidays, summer, family and friends. I love barbecuing so much that I've probably tried to cook just about everything on the barbecue at one time or another! When the weather is good, I'll build a fire at home and cook on the barbecue every couple of nights. It's definitely my favourite cooking technique as it adds depth of flavour with the smokiness and caramelisation. One of my favourite things to do is push the barbecue to the side and just build a fire in an old drum, put a rack on top and cook on that. Every year when I go on holidays to the river at Echuca with my mates, I build a barbecue in a fire pit. It's all about building happy memories and food is an important part of that.

If you're entertaining around the barbecue and you give someone a barbecued sausage in bread they'll probably wander off and eat it. However, if you put a whole butterflied chicken in the middle of the table with a few exciting sides and salads around it, people will want to stay at the table and enjoy time together. They'll talk about the food and the interesting flavours and you'll find yourself at the table a lot longer with the people who mean the most to you.

From pulled pork tacos to barbecued pizzas, this chapter is a smoky-food lover's dream. And to serve with your barbecue, I've included ideas for fresh salads with enticing flavours and textural contrasts.

HONEY SESAME
CHICKEN SKEWERS

SERVES 4

4 bamboo or metal skewers
600 g skinless chicken thigh
  fillets, cut into thick strips
8 kaffir lime leaves
2 tablespoons honey
2 tablespoons sesame seeds
large handful coriander leaves
lime wedges to serve

MARINADE
80 ml (⅓ cup) fish sauce
1 tablespoon dried chilli flakes
3 cm piece of ginger, peeled
  and grated
2 lemongrass stems, white
  part only, finely chopped
  and crushed using a mortar
  and pestle
1 teaspoon ground turmeric
2 garlic cloves, grated

You can play around with the flavours in this recipe to cater for your own tastebuds. I like to add some extra chilli as I'm a new-found chilli aficionado. These go well with Thai cabbage and snow pea salad with honey peanuts (page 116).

Soak the bamboo skewers in cold water for 20–30 minutes.

Combine all the marinade ingredients in a bowl and add the chicken and a little salt and pepper. Mix well to combine. Set aside to marinate in the refrigerator for at least 30 minutes.

Preheat the barbecue to high.

Thread the pieces of marinated chicken onto the skewers, alternating with the lime leaves. You should end up with about 3 pieces of chicken per skewer.

Once the barbecue is smoking hot, add the chicken skewers and cook over high heat to get as much caramelisation as possible. Don't stress if the chicken is burning – it adds great flavour, as long as they are not completely black. Turn them 5 or 6 times every minute or two for 4–5 minutes. Once the chicken is almost cooked, turn off the heat then drizzle over the honey and sprinkle over the sesame seeds. Flip the skewers a couple more times and let the remaining heat of the barbecue toast the honey and sesame seeds.

Serve immediately with the coriander and a squeeze of lime juice.

BRENT'S TIP: Ensure the heat is off when the honey is added, otherwise it will burn really quickly.

BARBECUED PRAWNS
WITH CHILLI JAM

SERVES 4

12 raw tiger prawns, peeled and deveined, tails intact
4 metal skewers
2 limes, halved, plus 2 limes for serving
80 g (¼ cup) Thai chilli jam (page 29), plus extra to serve

These prawns can be prepared and eaten within 15 minutes! If you're feeling a little adventurous, leave the shells on the prawns - it keeps the meat juicier and adds a great crunch. Serve this with Thai cabbage and snow pea salad with honey peanuts (page 116).

Heat the barbecue to medium–high.

Thread 3 prawns onto each skewer.

Place the halved limes, cut side down, on the barbecue and cook for 1–2 minutes until lightly caramelised.

Barbecue the prawn skewers for 1 minute on each side. Brush the prawns with a thick layer of the chilli jam and cook for about 30–60 seconds more on each side, or until the prawns are just cooked through.

Serve the prawns with a squeeze of lime and the extra chilli jam.

BRENT'S TIP: Keep the heads and shells of the prawns. Roast them, then use them to make a beautiful stock.

BARBECUED BUTTERFLIED SPICED CHOOK

SERVES 4

1.8 kg free-range chicken
270 g (1 cup) Jerk spice rub
   (page 28)
olive oil for cooking
½ fresh pineapple, peeled
   and cut into 1.5 cm slices
1 lemon, halved

Butterflying a chicken means you get a lot more charring and caramelisation all over. The jerk marinade is hot, so serve this with a refreshing salad like Celeriac and apple slaw (page 112).

Place the chicken, breast side down, on a chopping board. Using chicken scissors, cut the chicken along either side of the backbone and then remove it. Spread the chicken flat, flip it over and press your palm onto the breastbone to flatten or butterfly the chook. Put the chicken into a large container, spoon over 200 g (¾ cup) of the jerk spice rub. Rub it into the chicken, cover and place in the refrigerator to marinate for a few hours or preferably overnight. When ready to cook, remove the chicken from the container and rub off any excess marinade and discard it.

Preheat the barbecue to medium.

Season the chicken with salt and a dash of olive oil, then place it on the grill plate, breast side down. Cook for 15 minutes and then flip it over. Brush over a little of the reserved marinade and cook, covered, for a further 15 minutes. Brush another layer of marinade on the chicken, turn the heat up to medium–high and cook for 2–3 minutes to caramelise the chicken. Check for doneness by inserting a skewer into the thickest part of the thigh – the juices should run clear. Remove the chicken from the barbecue and let it rest, covered loosely with foil, for at least 20 minutes.

Brush the pineapple lightly with olive oil and grill it on the barbecue for 3–4 minutes each side, until caramelised and just cooked through. Squeeze the lemon over the top of the chicken and serve with the grilled pineapple.

BRENT'S TIP: Be careful not to have your barbecue on too high a heat as the marinade will burn easily.

DIG IN!

STEAK BURGER
WITH PANCETTA, SMOKED CHEDDAR AND SMOKED TOMATO RELISH

MAKES 4

4 thin slices pancetta
2 tablespoons olive oil, plus extra for cooking
2 large onions, thinly sliced
1 tablespoon sugar
2 garlic cloves, crushed
4 x 150 g scotch fillet steaks
4 slices smoked cheddar cheese
4 burger buns
95 g (⅓ cup) Smoked tomato relish (page 32)
handful rocket or baby English spinach leaves
100 g (⅓ cup) Chipotle mayo (page 23)

This is very rich dude food, especially when served with the Eggplant chips with spicy kewpie mayo (page 69). To lighten it up a little, remove the onion and add some pickles instead.

Preheat the barbecue to high.

Cook the pancetta on the barbecue grill plate until caramelised, about 30–60 seconds each side. Or, alternatively, cook it in a small frying pan over medium–high heat. Set aside. Reduce the heat on the barbecue to low and add the 2 tablespoons of oil and onions. Sprinkle with the sugar and cook for 15 minutes, without colouring. Add the garlic and cook for a further 10 minutes. Alternatively, cook in a small frying pan over medium heat. Remove the onion mixture and transfer to paper towel to drain.

Season the steaks with salt and pepper and a dash of olive oil.

Turn the barbecue to high again. Once the barbecue is smoking, add the steaks. Cook for 2–3 minutes then flip over, cover with the cheese and cook for a further 2 minutes. Remove and rest, covered, in a warm place.

While the steak is resting, slice the burger buns in half and place them on the grill, cut side down, to toast for about 30–60 seconds. (Only toast the cut side.)

Remove the toasted buns from the barbecue and assemble your burger. Spread the tomato relish on the bottom bun, then top with the caramelised onion, steak, pancetta and rocket. Finish with the chipotle mayo then top with the other half of the bun.

PULLED PORK TACOS

SERVES 4–6

PULLED PORK

2 kg bone-in pork shoulder, skin removed and excess fat trimmed

300 g (4–5 cups) hickory smoking chips (largest pieces), soaked in water for 30 minutes before use

250 ml (1 cup) dry cider

250 ml (1 cup) white wine vinegar

2 onions, roughly chopped

1 garlic bulb, cloves separated and bruised

DRY RUB

2 tablespoons brown sugar

1 tablespoon cayenne pepper

1 teaspoon salt

1 teaspoon freshly ground black pepper

1 teaspoon dried chilli flakes

1 teaspoon smoked paprika

dash of olive oil

There's nothing like slow-cooked smoky pork that just falls off the bone and melts in your mouth. Put it in a taco with a delicious textural salad and it's the ultimate! As well as the Mexican barbecued corn salad, try it with Haloumi and mint salad (page 113) or Celeriac and apple slaw (page 112).

For the pulled pork, heat the coals in a kettle barbecue.

For the dry rub, mix all the ingredients together until well combined. Rub the mixture over the pork, ensuring you coat the meat evenly.

Strain the wood chips and place them on top of the preheated coals in the barbecue.

In a large tray, combine the cider, vinegar, onions, garlic and 250 ml (1 cup) water. Place on the rack in the barbecue above the coals and place a meat rack over the tray.

Place the pork on the meat rack and cook over very low heat for a minimum of 4 hours. Check the tray after 1½ hours to ensure the moisture hasn't evaporated. Top up with a little water if required.

After about 4 hours, check the pork – it should be falling off the bone and you should be able to pull it apart easily with 2 forks. If it's ready, remove it from the barbecue and rest, covered with foil, for at least 20 minutes. If it isn't soft enough, cook it for a further 20 minutes and keep testing until it's done.

TACOS

12 large flour tortillas either
　homemade (see page 25)
　or store-bought
Mexican barbecued corn salad
　(page 112) to serve
1 large avocado, sliced
250 g (1 cup) sour cream
large handful coriander leaves

Shred the pork meat using 2 forks and place it in a shallow pan with half the strained cooking liquid from the tray under the pork. This will ensure the pork is juicy.

Reduce the barbecue heat to medium.

For the tacos, wrap the tortillas in foil and heat in the barbecue for 5–10 minutes before serving.

Assemble the tacos starting with a good spoonful of the Mexican barbecued corn salad, followed by some avocado and pulled pork topped with sour cream and fresh coriander.

BRENT'S TIPS: Cooking the pork can be so simple. If you don't have a kettle barbecue, you can cook it in the oven. Use the same methods but have your oven at 170°C (or 150°C for a fan-forced oven). Cover the pork with foil for the first 4 hours, then remove the foil and bake for a further hour. Leave out the woodchips!

Cooking times for every barbecue will vary due to temperature control. Try to have the heat as low as possible and check your pork after 3 hours. Boneless pork will cook quicker but have less flavour.

PULLED PORK TACOS WITH
MEXICAN BARBECUED
CORN SALAD

AMERICAN-STYLE STICKY PORK RIBS

SERVES 4

2 x 375 ml bottles dry cider
125 ml (½ cup) cider vinegar
2 large racks (1.4 kg in total)
   pork ribs

DRY RUB
1 tablespoon onion powder
1 tablespoon garlic powder
1 tablespoon cayenne pepper

MARINADE
1 x 375 ml can Coca-Cola
125 ml (½ cup) tomato sauce
125 ml (½ cup) dry apera
   (sherry)
55 g (¼ cup) brown sugar
3 garlic cloves, crushed
2 tablespoons Tabasco sauce

Ribs are 'fingers only' food. They're messy, fun, sticky and damn good. Adding the Coca-Cola gives the ribs a complex molasses sweetness and this intensifies and caramelises when cooked. Yum! This is comfort food, so carry on the vibe and serve with Wedges with blue cheese sauce (page 68) or Perfect chips (page 24).

Preheat a barbecue to high with the hood closed.

Combine the dry rub ingredients in a bowl.

Put the cider, cider vinegar and 500 ml (2 cups) water in a large roasting dish and place a roasting rack on top. Dust the ribs lightly with the dry rub then place them on the roasting rack. Cover tightly with foil and cook on the barbecue for 1 hour.

Meanwhile, place all the marinade ingredients in a large saucepan over medium heat and cook for 20 minutes or until thickened, stirring every few minutes.

Remove the ribs from the barbecue and discard the liquid. Brush on a thick layer of the marinade. Place the ribs directly on the barbecue over medium heat and grill to char the outside. Cook until both sides are charred, about 5–10 minutes, brushing with the marinade and turning every few minutes.

Alternatively, cook the ribs in a 160°C oven (or 140°C for a fan-forced oven) for 1 hour. Transfer the ribs to a roasting tin, increase the oven temperature to 220°C (or 200°C for a fan-forced oven), brush with the marinade and cook for 15–20 minutes, turning the ribs over every 5 minutes.

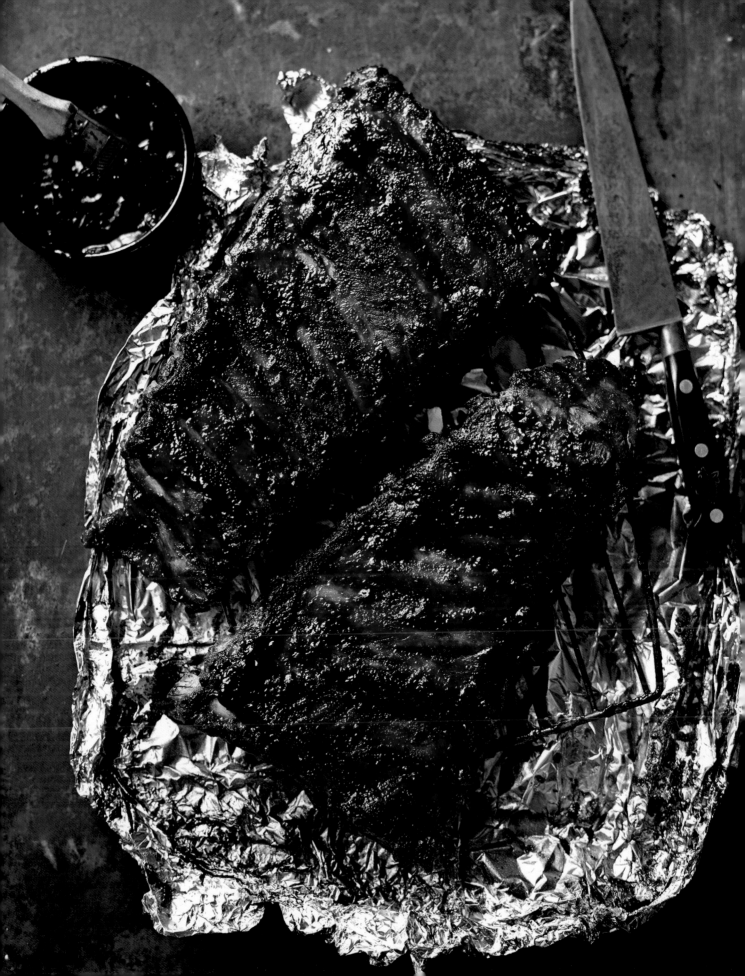

WHOLE THAI BARBECUED SNAPPER

SERVES 4

1.5 kg whole snapper, scaled and gutted
2 lemongrass stems, white part only, cut into 5 cm lengths
4 garlic cloves, peeled
10 kaffir lime leaves
roots and stems of 1 bunch coriander, washed, leaves reserved for garnish
3 cm piece galangal or ginger, peeled and roughly sliced
5 spring onions, thinly sliced

SAUCE
juice of 4 limes
60 ml (¼ cup) fish sauce
90 g (¼ cup) grated or shaved palm sugar
3 bird's eye chillies, thinly sliced
2 tablespoons peanut oil
2 tablespoons soy sauce

You can buy snapper fillets off the bone but when you've cooked a whole fish on the bone, you'll never go back to just cooking a fillet. The flavour is something else. Gutting and scaling a fish isn't as scary as you think. Don't be freaked out about trying new things because once you've tried it the first time, it gets easier each time. Remember with Asian food that it's all about the balance of flavours - sweet, salty, sour, hot. Taste and adjust to suit your palate. Serve with Thai cabbage and snow pea salad with honey peanuts (page 116).

Preheat the barbecue to high with the hood closed.

Rinse the fish, inside and out, under cold running water. Pat dry with paper towel.

Using the back of a knife, gently hit the lemongrass to bruise it. Place the lemongrass, garlic, lime leaves, coriander roots and stems and galangal in the cavity of the fish.

Make 3 slices, 1 cm deep and 5 cm apart, in the thickest part of both sides of the fish.

Tear off a large piece of aluminium foil (larger than the fish) and lay it flat on a work surface. Do the same with a piece of baking paper. Lay the baking paper on top of the foil then place the fish on top of the baking paper. Season the fish with salt and pepper.

Tear off another piece of foil a little larger than the first. Cover the fish loosely and crimp the edges to seal the fish inside.

Place the parcel in the barbecue and cook, with the hood closed, for 15 minutes. Flip the parcel over and cook for a further 10 minutes.

Remove the fish and leave it to rest, still wrapped in the foil, for 4–5 minutes. Unwrap the fish to check if it's done. Once you peel the flesh away, the bones should still be blushing pink and slightly opaque.

For the sauce, bring all the ingredients to the boil in a small saucepan over medium heat. Once boiling, cook for a further minute.

Gently pour the sauce over the cooked fish – pouring boiling liquid over the skin, stops it from having a rubbery consistency. Garnish with the reserved coriander leaves and the sliced spring onions.

BARBECUED PIZZAS

**MAKES 4 PIZZAS
(ALL TOPPINGS MAKE
ENOUGH FOR 1 PIZZA)**

PIZZA DOUGH
600 g (4 cups) high protein/
  baker's flour or plain flour,
  plus extra for dusting
2 teaspoons (7 g sachet)
  dried yeast
1 teaspoon salt
400 ml warm water
30 ml olive oil, plus olive
  oil spray
semolina flour for dusting

Not everybody can afford a pizza oven, so why not use the barbecue? The sky's the limit when it comes to toppings and there's no right or wrong way to top a pizza, so get creative. I've provided a recipe if you want to make your own pizza dough, but you can use store-bought pizza bases if you prefer.

Combine the flour, yeast and salt in a large bowl. Make a well in the centre and pour in the water and olive oil. Mix until combined, then cover the bowl with plastic wrap and set aside for 10 minutes. Turn the dough out onto a lightly floured surface and knead for 4–5 minutes until quite smooth and elastic. Place the dough in a clean bowl lightly oiled with olive oil, cover with plastic wrap and set aside in a warm place for 30–60 minutes until it has doubled in size.

Punch the dough down gently, dust the work surface lightly with semolina and knead the dough a couple of times until smooth. Divide into 4 and shape into balls. Set aside on a tray dusted with semolina for 10 minutes to rest.

Preheat a barbecue with a hood to medium. Spray a 30 cm square of foil lightly with olive oil spray.

Roll and stretch one of the dough balls on a lightly floured surface to dinner plate-size (about 24 cm in diameter). Place the foil square on a tray (for easy transport to the barbecue), dust with semolina, put the pizza dough base on the foil, then add your choice of toppings. (See opposite.)

Slide the foil with the pizza carefully off the tray, directly onto the barbecue grill and cook, with the lid closed, for 10–12 minutes, or until the base is cooked through and the topping is lightly browned. Alternatively, preheat the oven to 230°C (or 210°C for a fan-forced oven) and cook the pizza on an oven tray or pizza stone for 12–15 minutes or until the base is cooked through and the top is lightly browned. Repeat with the remaining dough balls.

TOPPINGS

CHEESE STEAK PIZZA

1 garlic clove, crushed

70 g (¼ cup) cheese spread

¼ small brown onion, thinly sliced

¼ small green capsicum, thinly sliced

100 g beef fillet or rump steak, in 3–4 mm slices

80 g grated provolone

3 small bocconcini balls

Mix the crushed garlic into the cheese spread, then spread it over the pizza dough base.

Top with a layer of onion and capsicum.

Top with slices of beef fillet and then sprinkle over the provolone cheese, allowing pieces of beef to poke through the cheese. Tear the bocconcini in half and dot it around the pizza. Season to taste.

Follow the directions for cooking the pizza opposite.

CHICKEN AND MANGO PIZZA

95 g (⅓ cup) Smoked tomato relish (page 32)

2 eschalots (French shallots), thinly sliced

1 garlic clove, crushed

small handful baby English spinach leaves

1 skinless chicken breast fillet, thinly sliced

70 g (¼ cup) store-bought mango chutney

50 g grated cheddar cheese

small handful basil leaves, torn

40 g (¼ cup) pine nuts

Spread the tomato relish over the pizza dough base.

Top with the eschalots, garlic and spinach, then top with the sliced chicken breast. Add dollops of the chutney then sprinkle over the cheese.

Follow the directions for cooking the pizza opposite. Remove the pizza from the barbecue and top with the torn basil leaves and pine nuts.

ANTIPASTO PIZZA

95 g (⅓ cup) Smoked tomato relish (page 32)

¼ red capsicum, thinly sliced

1 eschalot (French shallot), thinly sliced

1 pickled artichoke heart, halved

1 tablespoon pitted whole black olives

1 tablespoon capers

3 anchovy fillets, halved

50 g blue cheese (I use King Island Roaring Forties)

5 slices prosciutto

50 g (⅓ cup) grated mozzarella

10 baby pickled onions, halved

small handful chopped flat-leaf parsley

small handful rocket leaves

Spread the relish over the pizza dough base. Top with the capsicum, eschalot, artichoke, olives, capers, anchovies and blue cheese. Drape pieces of the prosciutto over the top and sprinkle with the grated mozzarella.

Follow the directions for cooking the pizza opposite. Remove the pizza from the barbecue, then top with the pickled onion halves, parsley and rocket.

BARBECUED PIZZAS LEFT TO RIGHT: ANTIPASTO;
CHICKEN AND MANGO; CHEESE STEAK

VIETNAMESE LETTUCE CUPS

SERVES 4

---

1 iceberg lettuce
150 g chicken mince
150 g pork mince
2 cm piece ginger, peeled and
    grated
1 garlic clove, grated
2 eschalots (French shallots),
    grated
60 ml (¼ cup) fish sauce
2 tablespoons peanut oil, plus
    1 extra teaspoon
handful roasted, unsalted
    peanuts
100 g rice vermicelli noodles
2 large round rice paper
    wrappers (banh trang)
100 g enoki mushrooms,
    separated
180 g (2 cups) bean sprouts
1 small Lebanese cucumber,
    cut into batons
1 carrot, peeled and julienned
handful Vietnamese mint or
    mint, torn
handful coriander leaves,
    roughly chopped
3 long red chillies, thinly
    sliced
lime cheeks to serve

This is great sharing food and a guaranteed crowd-pleaser. Guests assemble the cups themselves, so it's fun as well as being delicious. It's hard to go wrong – I love heaps of mint, coriander and lime, but build the flavours to suit your taste.

Peel individual leaves off the lettuce, trying not to tear them. Rinse them thoroughly to remove any grit.

In a large bowl combine the chicken mince, pork mince, ginger, garlic, eschalots and fish sauce. Season with salt and pepper then combine together thoroughly with clean hands.

Place a wok over the highest heat possible. When it is smoking add half the peanut oil. Add half of the mince mixture and stir-fry constantly until crumbly and golden brown.

Transfer the mixture to a sieve over a bowl and strain out any remaining liquid. Discard the liquid. Repeat the process with the remaining 1 tablespoon of oil and mince.

Reduce the heat to medium, add the peanuts to the wok and fry until lightly coloured, about 1–2 minutes.

Meanwhile, put the noodles in a bowl and cover with boiling water. After 2 minutes, or when the noodles are tender, drain well.

In a frying pan over high heat, fry the dry rice paper wrappers in the extra teaspoon of oil, one at a time, until toasted, about 1–2 minutes. Once cooked, break them up into pieces to fit into the lettuce cups.

On a platter, make a stack of your rice paper pieces, then a stack of lettuce cups, the individual salad items (mushrooms, bean sprouts, cucumber and carrot), a bowl of the mince mixture, the toasted peanuts, the mint and coriander, the chilli, the lime and the noodles.

CELERIAC AND APPLE SLAW

SERVES 4

100 g (1 cup) walnuts,
  chopped
1 celeriac
2 granny smith apples
60 ml (¼ cup) dry cider
15 g (½ cup) thinly sliced
  flat-leaf parsley
2 tablespoons Parsley mayo
  (page 23)

People don't cook with celeriac that much, but it's soooo good! This slaw can be eaten with a range of foods or is delicious on its own. Serve it as a side with barbecued meats, put it in your tacos or quesadillas or add it to a chicken sandwich.

Toast the walnuts in a large dry frying pan over medium–high heat for 4–5 minutes or until fragrant. Set aside to cool.

Chop the celeriac and apples into julienne, or use a mandoline if you have one. Combine with the remaining ingredients and let sit for 15 minutes to let the flavours infuse and develop before eating.

MEXICAN BARBECUED CORN SALAD

SERVES 4–6

3 corn cobs (husks removed)
1 large red onion, halved
3 fresh jalapeños
5 large ripe tomatoes, roughly
  chopped
1 bunch coriander, leaves
  roughly chopped, some
  sprigs reserved for serving
juice of 3 limes
100 g (⅔ cup) cotija or
  crumbled feta cheese

Charring the corn gives this simple salad an extra smoky dimension and the corn also provides some crunch.

For the barbecued corn salad, bring a large saucepan of water to the boil over medium heat. Add the corn cobs and boil for 3 minutes, until just tender. Remove and drain well.

Place the onion and jalapeños directly over the flame on your cooktop or barbecue and cook until blackened all over, about 8–10 minutes. Transfer to a bowl, cover with plastic wrap and allow them to steam in their own heat for a further 5–10 minutes. Remove the plastic wrap and allow to cool.

Cook the corn until lightly charred on all sides either on the barbecue or in a chargrill pan over high heat, about 4–5 minutes.

Remove and set aside to cool. Once the blackened ingredients have cooled down, peel off the charred skins, reserving the smoky inner flesh. Roughly chop the jalapeños and finely dice the onion.

Once the corn has cooled, lay it flat on a board and cut away the kernels using a sharp knife. Combine the corn with the onion, tomato, jalapeño and chopped coriander in a large salad bowl. Squeeze over the lime juice, crumble over the cheese and top with the coriander sprigs.

HALOUMI AND MINT SALAD

SERVES 4–6

100 g (½ cup) red quinoa, rinsed and drained
250 g haloumi cheese, sliced 1 cm thick
juice of 2 lemons
60 ml (¼ cup) olive oil
1 bunch mint leaves, finely shredded
½ bunch flat-leaf parsley, chopped
100 g rocket leaves

PICKLED ESCHALOTS
60 ml (¼ cup) red wine vinegar
2 tablespoons white sugar
2 eschalots (French shallots), finely diced

Eat this fresh as the haloumi won't retain its gooey texture once cold. Put a pile of this on barbecued lamb while it's resting to infuse the meat with the delicious flavours.

For the pickled eschalots, put the vinegar, 60 ml (¼ cup) water and the sugar in a small saucepan over medium heat. Bring to the boil then remove from the heat and add the eschalots. Set aside and allow to pickle in the liquid until cool.

Put the quinoa and 250 ml (1 cup) water in a medium saucepan over medium heat. Bring to the boil, then reduce the heat to low and cook, covered, for 12 minutes or until tender. The water will be absorbed. Remove the pan from the heat, remove the lid and allow to sit for 5 minutes. Fluff the quinoa up with a fork and set aside to cool.

Put a chargrill pan over high heat. When hot cook the haloumi for 2 minutes on each side or until golden. Transfer to baking paper and squeeze over the juice of 1 lemon.

Whisk together the remaining lemon juice and the olive oil until well incorporated. Season with salt and pepper. Taste the dressing – it should be very tangy.

Drain the eschalots and combine with the quinoa, herbs and rocket. Drizzle on the dressing then top with the haloumi. Serve immediately.

CHARRED SWEET
ONION SALAD

SERVES 4

2 tablespoons olive oil
8 baby onions, halved
  lengthways but not peeled
20 g butter
80 g (½ cup) almonds
2 teaspoons honey
250 ml (1 cup) apple cider
  vinegar
220 g (1 cup) sugar
10 asparagus spears, trimmed
60 g rocket leaves
6 slices prosciutto
3 baby cucumbers or
  1 Lebanese cucumber
60 g baby English spinach
  leaves
2 ripe pears, peeled, cored
  and cut into small wedges
100 g goat's cheese, crumbled

DRESSING
zest and juice of 1 lemon
60 ml (¼ cup) olive oil
1 teaspoon dijon mustard

This salad has a strong salt hit from the cheese and prosciutto, acid from the lemon, sweetness from the honey-glazed almonds and smokiness from the charred onions. The juicy pear and cucumber add a refreshing note.

Put the olive oil in a large frying pan over high heat and season the oil with salt. Place the onions, cut side down, in an even layer around the frying pan. Cook for 6–7 minutes then add the butter and cover the pan. Cook for a further 5 minutes. Remove the onions from the pan and set aside to cool.

Wipe out the frying pan with paper towel then place it back over medium heat. Add the almonds and cook until lightly golden, about 3–4 minutes. Add the honey and cook for a further minute, tossing to coat the nuts, then remove them from the heat. Transfer them to a plate, set aside to cool down slightly.

In a large saucepan over high heat, put the vinegar, sugar and 125 ml (½ cup) water. Bring to the boil then remove the pan from the heat. Remove the outer skin of the cooled onions and put them in the liquid. Set them aside to cool down in the liquid for at least 30 minutes.

Bring a small saucepan of water to the boil over high heat. Add the asparagus and cook for 2–3 minutes. Remove and transfer straight to iced water to halt the cooking process.

Wipe out the frying pan with paper towel, set it over medium heat and add the prosciutto. Cook it until caramelised and crispy then transfer to paper towel. Add the asparagus to the same pan and cook over high heat for 2–3 minutes. Remove the asparagus from the pan and slice the spears in half lengthways.

For the dressing, in a bowl, whisk all the ingredients together until incorporated. Slice the cucumbers in half then remove the seeds with a spoon. Slice the cucumber into 2 cm chunks, combine them with the remaining ingredients, except the almonds and goat's cheese. Drizzle over the dressing and top with the almonds and crumbled cheese.

THAI CABBAGE
AND SNOW PEA SALAD WITH HONEY PEANUTS

SERVES 6

350 g cabbage, finely
  shredded
5 spring onions, cut into
  5 cm lengths
1 carrot, cut into finger-sized
  batons
100 g (1 cup) snow peas, finely
  shredded
90 g (1 cup) bean sprouts
1 bunch coriander leaves

HONEY PEANUTS
80 g (½ cup) roasted peanuts
1 teaspoon honey

DRESSING
1 tablespoon fish sauce
1 tablespoon shaved palm
  sugar
1 bird's eye chilli, thinly sliced
  (seeded if you don't want it
  too hot)
juice of 1 lime

This dish represents a vegetarian me on a plate (well, apart from the fish sauce)! This is one of my favourites that I eat at least once a week. It's so fresh and includes my beloved Southeast Asian flavours. Peanuts are crunchy but turn creamy as you chew them. This salad goes really well with barbecued meats or even in lettuce cups. It's full of flavours and textures to stimulate the senses.

For the honey peanuts, put the peanuts in a large dry frying pan over medium heat and cook until golden, about 5 minutes – be careful not to burn them. Once golden, add the honey and toss to coat. Remove from the pan and set aside.

For the dressing, combine the fish sauce and palm sugar in a small bowl and stir until the sugar dissolves. Add the chilli and lime juice and combine. Check for a good balance of flavours and adjust as necessary.

Combine all the salad ingredients, except the honey peanuts and coriander. Drizzle over the dressing and top with the honey peanuts and fresh coriander leaves.

ROAST PUMPKIN
AND PINE NUT SALAD

SERVES 6

1 large butternut pumpkin, unpeeled, halved lengthways and seeds reserved
1 tablespoon olive oil
1 teaspoon smoked paprika
80 g (½ cup) pine nuts
90 ml (¼ cup) honey
small handful long green beans
120 g rocket leaves
120 g baby English spinach leaves
100 g feta cheese, crumbled

BALSAMIC DRESSING
60 ml (¼ cup) balsamic vinegar
60 ml (¼ cup) olive oil

You don't need 20 ingredients in a salad - just a few different flavours as well as textures for interest and contrast. The green beans add crunch here.

Preheat the oven to 220°C (or 200°C for a fan-forced oven).

Slice the pumpkin into 2 cm slices, season with salt and pepper and drizzle over the olive oil. Lay the pumpkin flat on a large baking tray and roast in the oven for 30 minutes.

After 30 minutes, sprinkle over the paprika and cook the pumpkin for a further 10 minutes. Remove the pumpkin from the oven and allow to cool to room temperature.

Put the pine nuts in a small dry frying pan over medium heat and fry for about 3–4 minutes until golden brown. Add the honey and cook for 2 more minutes, stirring to coat until sticky, then remove from the heat.

In a medium saucepan over high heat, bring 500 ml (2 cups) water to the boil. Season the water then add the beans. Cook the beans for 2–3 minutes until bright green but still with some crunch, then transfer to a bowl of iced water. Set aside until serving.

For the dressing, in a small bowl whisk together the vinegar and olive oil. Season and taste to check the balance of flavours – it should be quite acidic.

Assemble the salad by combining the rocket and spinach leaves in a bowl. Add the pumpkin and beans and drizzle over the dressing. Top with the pine nuts and crumbled feta cheese and serve.

FREEKEH SALAD
WITH ALMONDS AND POMEGRANATE

SERVES 4–6

165 g (1 cup) cracked freekeh, rinsed

500 ml (2 cups) vegetable stock or water

½ teaspoon cumin seeds

few drops of rosewater

2 spring onions, thinly sliced

seeds of 1 pomegranate

60 g (½ cup) slivered almonds

½ teaspoon sumac

1 long red chilli, finely diced

1 bunch flat-leaf parsley leaves, finely chopped

1 bunch mint leaves, torn

1 garlic clove, crushed

60 ml (¼ cup) olive oil

juice of 2 lemons

Freekeh is a superfood that's high in fibre, cheap and very easy to cook and it's available at the supermarket. It can be used in salads or tossed with some vegetables for dinner. This Middle Eastern-inspired salad makes a great vegetarian meal on its own, but is also great served with barbecued meats.

Put the freekeh, stock, cumin seeds and rosewater in a large saucepan over high heat. Bring to the boil then reduce the heat to medium–low and cook, covered, until the liquid is absorbed and the freekeh is just tender, about 20 minutes.

Tip the freekeh out onto a tray and spread it in an even layer to cool.

Combine all the ingredients in a bowl and season with salt and pepper. Check for seasoning and whether there is enough acidity from the lemon – it should be slightly tangy. Adjust as necessary and serve.

BRENT'S TIP: If you use uncracked freekeh, you will need to increase the cooking time to around 50 minutes.

BALSAMIC ROASTED BEETROOT
AND GOAT'S CHEESE SALAD

SERVES 4

1 bunch (about 12) baby
   beetroot
zest and juice of 2 oranges
60 ml (¼ cup) balsamic
   vinegar
2 tablespoons olive oil
2 tablespoons sugar
50 g (½ cup) walnuts
60 g baby English spinach
   leaves
150 g goat's cheese, crumbled

There are only a few ingredients in this salad but it's a cracker.
The beetroot is the hero, there's creamy tangy goat's cheese
and there are walnuts for crunch.

Preheat the oven to 200°C (or 180°C for a fan-forced oven).

Trim the beetroot stalks to about 2 cm long and wash the beetroot
very well to remove any grit and dirt in the stem. Pat dry.

Combine the orange zest and juice, vinegar, olive oil, sugar and salt
to season in a small roasting tin. Add the beetroot and toss to coat.
Cover with foil and roast for 35 minutes. After 35 minutes, remove
the foil and continue to cook for 10 more minutes.

Remove the beetroot from the oven and set aside to cool. Reserve
the pan juices. Slice the beetroot in half lengthways, leaving some
whole if you like.

In a small frying pan over low heat, dry-fry the walnuts for
2–3 minutes, tossing continuously until toasted and golden.

Put the spinach leaves in a large bowl. Add the cooled beetroot
with its pan juices, then top with the walnuts and goat's cheese.

BRENT'S TIP: When chopping beetroot, put some baking paper on
your chopping board to protect it. Beetroot stains everything it touches.

NEW CLASSICS

I love reinventing dishes and this chapter is full of classics and old-fashioned favourites to which I've added my own personal twists.

Of course, the term 'classic' means something different to everyone. Someone like me, who grew up in Australia, will have a very different idea of 'classic' from someone who grew up in Morocco or China. But in this chapter I've included the recipes that I remember from my childhood – the dishes that my mum and dad would cook for me and my sisters. I've just updated them and added a few different flavours and cooking techniques here and there to make them a bit more interesting – although Mum and Dad might still claim that their versions are better!

I love hearty home-cooked food and this chapter contains many recipes that might take you back to your own childhood, from warming soups and slow-cooked stews to curried sausages and chicken parmigiana.

POTATO AND LEEK SOUP
WITH BACON AND CHIVES

SERVES 4

40 g unsalted butter

2 leeks, white part only, thinly sliced

2 garlic cloves, roughly chopped

¼ teaspoon freshly grated nutmeg

750 ml (3 cups) vegetable stock

3 large potatoes, washed and peeled, peel reserved

4 rashers bacon

125 ml (½ cup) pouring cream

white pepper

small bunch chives, finely chopped

This is a classic winter warmer but I've taken it to the next level by adding a few different textures on top. Watch you don't purée the potatoes too much or they will turn into a gluggy mess. I also use the potato skins for extra flavour.

Put the butter in a large saucepan over medium heat. When the butter has melted and is starting to foam, add the leeks and sweat for 6–8 minutes. Add the garlic and cook for a further 2 minutes, then add the nutmeg and stock. Bring to the boil.

Tie the potato skins in a piece of muslin. Grate the potatoes and add both the skins and grated potato to the pan. Bring the mixture to the boil then reduce the heat to low and allow to simmer, covered, for 12 minutes, until tender. Remove the potato skins from the pan and discard.

Meanwhile, turn the grill to high.

Put the bacon on an oven tray and grill until crispy. Remove and transfer to paper towel to absorb any excess oil, then crumble.

Blitz the potato mixture with a hand-held blender until smooth. Add half the cream and blitz again to incorporate. Season with salt and white pepper and transfer to serving bowls. Ripple through the remaining cream, top with the crunchy bacon, garnish with the chives and serve.

INDIAN SPICY CAULIFLOWER SOUP

SERVES 4–6

1½ large cauliflowers
1 tablespoon vegetable oil
½ teaspoon ground cumin
40 g ghee
1 large brown onion, finely
  diced
3 cm piece ginger, peeled
  and finely chopped
3 garlic cloves, crushed
½ teaspoon ground turmeric
½ teaspoon chilli powder
½ teaspoon garam masala
250 ml (1 cup) vegetable stock
10 curry leaves
125 g (½ cup) natural Greek-
  style yoghurt
handful coriander leaves

This soup has as much flavour as any main. It's a winner on cold rainy days, served with crusty bread or poppadoms.

Preheat the oven to 200°C (or 180°C for a fan-forced oven).

Cut the florets off half of the whole cauliflower, trying to get them roughly the same size. Reserve the stalk for the soup. Put the florets on a roasting tray and add 1 teaspoon of the vegetable oil, the cumin and some salt and pepper. Toss to coat then roast in the oven for 20–25 minutes until browned and tender.

Put the ghee in a large saucepan over medium heat. Once melted, add the onion and sweat for 5–6 minutes. Add the ginger and garlic and cook, stirring every minute, for 2–3 minutes. Add the turmeric, chilli powder and garam masala and cook for a further minute. Thinly slice the cauliflower stalk and remaining cauliflower and add it to the pan along with the vegetable stock. Bring to the boil then reduce the heat to medium–low, cover and cook for 15–20 minutes, until tender.

Meanwhile, heat the remaining oil in a small frying pan over high heat. Add the curry leaves, but stand back because they might spit, and fry for 30 seconds. Remove and transfer to paper towel to absorb any excess oil.

Once the soup base has cooked, remove the pan from the heat, allow to cool for a minute or two, then blitz with a hand-held blender until smooth. Add half the yoghurt and blitz again. Taste for seasoning. Serve in deep bowls, topped with the remaining yoghurt, the fried curry leaves, the roasted cauliflower florets and the coriander leaves.

THAI PUMPKIN SOUP
WITH CORIANDER

SERVES 4

1 butternut pumpkin (about 2 kg), peeled, grated and seeds reserved

olive oil for drizzling

2 teaspoons caster sugar

1 tablespoon peanut oil

4 eschalots (French shallots), peeled and thinly sliced

2 cm piece ginger, peeled and thinly sliced

4 garlic cloves, thinly sliced

1 bunch coriander, leaves picked, stems thinly sliced

60 ml (¼ cup) tamarind purée

250 ml (1 cup) vegetable stock

125 ml (½ cup) coconut cream

fish sauce to taste

2 bird's eye chillies, very thinly sliced

4 spring onions, thinly sliced diagonally

2 kaffir lime leaves, finely shredded

This is a jazzed-up pumpkin soup and contains my favourite Southeast Asian flavours - lime, ginger, chilli, garlic and fish sauce. I've also included tamarind for a nice sour hit - I tend to add a little more than I have suggested here, as I love it!

Preheat the oven to 200°C (or 180°C for a fan-forced oven).

Ensure the pumpkin seeds are clean and are not covered with any pumpkin flesh. Put them on a baking tray, season them with salt and pepper, drizzle them with a dash of olive oil and bake in the oven until crisp and golden, around 10–15 minutes. Remove the tray from the oven and sprinkle the sugar over the seeds. Using a blowtorch, caramelise the sugar for 2–3 minutes or until the sugar is golden. Shake the tray to coat the seeds. Set aside. Alternatively, caramelise the seeds under a preheated medium–high grill for 2–3 minutes.

Add the peanut oil to a large saucepan over medium heat and fry the eschalots, ginger and garlic for 2–3 minutes. Add the coriander stems and sweat for a further minute. Add the grated pumpkin and the tamarind. Reduce the heat to medium–low, add the stock and cook, covered, for 12–15 minutes, shaking the pan every 5 minutes. Remove from the heat and allow to cool slightly.

Using a hand-held blender, blitz the pumpkin mixture in the pan until smooth. Add half the coconut cream and blitz again. Season with the fish sauce.

Transfer the soup to serving bowls, swirl through the remaining coconut cream, scatter over the chilli, spring onion, lime leaves and roasted pumpkin seeds and top with the coriander leaves.

RED LENTIL DAL
WITH COCONUT CREAM

3 large tomatoes
1 teaspoon mustard oil
1 brown onion, roughly
  chopped
1 tablespoon ghee
3 garlic cloves, crushed
3 cm piece ginger, peeled
  and finely chopped
½ teaspoon ground cumin
½ teaspoon coriander seeds
4 cardamom pods, lightly
  crushed
1 teaspoon ground turmeric
½ teaspoon garam masala
½ teaspoon chilli powder
1 teaspoon tomato paste
250 g (1 cup) red lentils
500 ml (2 cups) vegetable
  stock
125 ml (½ cup) coconut cream
1 bunch coriander, leaves
  picked

You can buy most of the flavouring ingredients for Indian food in the supermarket and they last for ages in the pantry. Lentils are a couple of dollars per packet and you can get four flavoursome dishes out of a packet. This creamy rich dal is great with plain steamed rice or flatbreads.

Preheat the oven to its highest temperature.

Slice the tomatoes in half, then in half again. Put them on a roasting tray, drizzle with a little mustard oil and season with salt. Roast them in the oven for 15 minutes. Remove and set aside to cool slightly.

Put the onion in a small food processor and blitz until smooth.

Put the ghee in a deep-sided frying pan or saucepan over medium heat. Add the pureed onion and sweat for 5–7 minutes but do not allow it to colour. Add the garlic and ginger and sweat for a further 2–3 minutes. Add the cumin, coriander seeds, cardamom pods, turmeric, garam masala and chilli powder and stir continuously to toast the spices, about 2–3 minutes. Add the tomato paste and stir for a further minute.

Put the roasted tomatoes in the food processor and blitz until they are smooth. Add them to the mixture in the frying pan and stir to combine.

Add the lentils and stock and increase the heat to high. Bring to the boil, reduce the heat to low, stir and then cook for 20–25 minutes, stirring occasionally, until the lentils are cooked – the mixture should be gluggy like a thick soup. Taste for seasoning.

Serve with a drizzle of coconut cream and garnish with coriander.

BEEF AND PORK MEATBALLS
IN SPICY TOMATO SAUCE

SERVES 4

300 g lean beef mince
200 g pork mince
3 garlic cloves, finely chopped
50 g (¼ cup) long-grain white
    rice
½ teaspoon dried oregano
1 egg, lightly beaten
15 g (½ cup) finely chopped
    flat-leaf parsley
30 g (½ cup) finely chopped
    basil, plus extra whole
    leaves for garnish
2 tablespoons olive oil
1 brown onion, chopped
3 anchovy fillets in oil, roughly
    chopped
1 teaspoon dried chilli flakes
50 g (¼ cup) capers
60 ml (¼ cup) red wine
    vinegar
400 g tinned chopped
    tomatoes
190 ml (¾ cup) tomato
    passata
pinch of sugar
100 g mozzarella, grated
100 g pecorino, grated
steamed rice to serve
crusty bread to serve

Meatballs are something I grew up eating. They're tasty, cheap and practically foolproof to make. I've accentuated the Italian flavours here by adding anchovies, capers and chilli.

In a large bowl, combine the beef and pork mince, half the garlic, the rice, oregano, egg, parsley and the chopped basil. Season with salt and pepper. Use your hands to combine the ingredients really well. Form walnut-sized meatballs.

Heat a large deep-sided, ovenproof frying pan over high heat and add 1 tablespoon of the olive oil. Add the meatballs to the pan and brown them on all sides, for about 5–6 minutes. Remove the meatballs from the pan and set aside.

Add the remaining oil to the pan, reduce the heat to medium, add the onion and cook for 4–5 minutes until soft. Add the remaining garlic, the anchovies, chilli flakes and capers and cook for a further minute. Add the red wine vinegar and cook for a further 3–4 minutes until the liquid has reduced. Add the tinned tomatoes and passata and season with the sugar. Bring to the boil then return the meatballs to the pan in an even layer. Cover the pan with a lid or foil and cook for 10–12 minutes. Remove the lid or foil, stir and cook for a further 5 minutes until cooked through.

Turn the grill to the highest heat.

Sprinkle the combined grated mozzarella and pecorino cheeses over the top of the meatballs and place the pan under the grill to melt and lightly brown the cheese. Alternatively, melt the cheese in the oven on 200°C (or 180°C for a fan-forced oven). Remove the pan from the grill, garnish with the whole basil leaves and serve. Serve with steamed rice and crusty bread.

CURRIED SAUSAGES

SERVES 4

2 teaspoons ghee
600 g beef sausages
2 brown onions, each cut into
  8 wedges
2 large garlic cloves, crushed
3 cm piece ginger, peeled and
  finely chopped
¼ teaspoon chilli powder
½ teaspoon curry powder
1 teaspoon garam masala
½ teaspoon ground cumin
4 new potatoes, washed and
  quartered
1 teaspoon tomato paste
400 g tinned diced tomatoes
250 ml (1 cup) vegetable stock
2 tablespoons natural yoghurt
coriander leaves to serve

Mum always made this dish when I was young, but it was simply sausages with potato, curry powder, peas and corn. I have dug deeper into the Indian roots of curry and incorporated a couple of other flavours like ghee, garlic, garam masala and cumin. Serve with steamed rice, Creamy mash (page 24) or flatbreads.

Put 1 teaspoon of the ghee in a large flameproof casserole dish over medium–high heat. When hot, add the sausages and sear until golden on all sides, about 5 minutes. Transfer to paper towel to absorb any excess oil.

Reduce the heat to medium–low and add the remaining ghee to the dish. When melted, add the onion and cook for 2 minutes. Add the garlic and ginger and cook for a further minute. Add the chilli powder, curry powder, garam masala and ground cumin and cook for a further 2 minutes, stirring constantly.

Add the potatoes to the pan and sauté until well coated in the spice mixture. Add the tomato paste and cook for a further minute. Add the tomatoes and mix well then add the stock.

Slice the sausages into thirds then return them to the pan. Cook, uncovered, for 15–20 minutes, until the sausages and potatoes are cooked through and the sauce has reduced and thickened.

Season to taste then swirl through the yoghurt, top with the coriander and serve.

BANGERS AND MASH
WITH MUSHROOM GRAVY

600 g thick beef sausages
35 g (¼ cup) plain flour
¼ teaspoon onion powder
¼ teaspoon garlic powder
2 eggs, lightly beaten
30 g (½ cup) panko crumbs
50 g (½ cup) dry breadcrumbs
125 ml (½ cup) vegetable oil
Creamy mash (page 24) to
   serve

MUSHROOM GRAVY
40 g butter
50 g Swiss brown mushrooms,
   thinly sliced
125 ml (½ cup) pouring cream
1 teaspoon worcestershire
   sauce

This recipe is my take on bangers and mash with some hardy flavours and crumbed sausages. I don't know if many people grew up eating crumbed sausages, but they were a staple at our house. Serve with the mash or with Gooey, cheesy potato balls (page 70) for a bit of deep-fried heaven.

Prick the sausages with a fork and add them to a large saucepan of water. Bring the water to the boil over high heat then cook for 8–10 minutes. Remove the sausages from the pan and allow to cool to room temperature.

Put the flour and onion and garlic powders in a small bowl. Put the beaten egg in a second bowl, and put the panko crumbs and breadcrumbs in a third.

Heat the vegetable oil in a large frying pan over medium heat.

Roll the sausages first in the flour mix, then the egg, then the breadcrumbs, then in the egg and breadcrumbs again, pressing the mixture onto the sausages to ensure the crumb stays on. Add the sausages to the frying pan and cook, turning regularly, until the crumb is golden brown all over, about 5–6 minutes. Transfer to paper towel to absorb any excess oil and season with salt.

For the mushroom gravy, put the butter in a small saucepan over medium heat. When foaming, add the mushrooms and cook for 3–5 minutes. Stir in the cream and worstershire sauce, taste for seasoning and cook for 2 minutes, until slightly thickened.

Serve the sausages on a bed of the creamy mash and drizzle over the mushroom gravy.

FISH BURGER
WITH LEMON AND BASIL MAYO

SERVES 4

75g (½ cup) plain flour
2 eggs, lightly beaten
60 g (1 cup) panko crumbs
½ teaspoon lemon pepper
vegetable oil for deep-frying
4 flathead fillets (about 320 g
  in total)
100 g (⅓ cup) Lemon and
  basil mayo (page 23)
4 long rolls, split two-thirds
  of the way through
4 small sweet-and-sour
  gherkins, sliced
handful flat-leaf parsley leaves
large handful rocket, rinsed
handful dill, chopped
sea salt to serve
lemon wedges to serve

PICKLED ESCHALOTS

60 ml (¼ cup) cider vinegar
55 g (¼ cup) sugar
1 tablespoon yellow mustard
  seeds
1 eschalot (French shallot),
  thinly sliced

This has all the familiar flavours of the fish shop – tartare sauce, gherkins, onion, lemon, basil and dill – but ramped up and reinvented as a burger. You have creaminess from the mayo, crunch from the crumbed fish, acid from the pickle and mustard, sweet and sour from the gherkin, and pepperiness from the rocket. It's a full-on flavour hit!

For the pickled eschalots, put 60 ml (¼ cup) water, the vinegar, sugar and mustard seeds in a small saucepan. Bring to the boil and remove the pan from the heat. Add the eschalot and set aside to let it cool and pickle in the liquid for at least 20 minutes. Transfer to paper towel to drain. Reserve some of the mustard seeds from the marinade for serving.

Put the flour, beaten egg and panko crumbs in 3 separate bowls. Season the crumbs with salt and the lemon pepper.

Fill a medium saucepan one-third full with vegetable oil. Set over medium heat and heat the oil. Alternatively, heat a deep-fryer to 180°C. Once the oil has reached 180°C on a thermometer or the oil bubbles around the handle of a wooden spoon dipped in it, dip the flathead fillets first in the flour, then the egg and then the panko crumbs, then dip in the egg and panko crumbs again for a double coating. Put the fillets into the hot oil and deep-fry them, in batches, until golden brown and cooked through, about 3–4 minutes. Transfer the fried fish to paper towel to absorb any excess oil.

Assemble your burgers. Spread a thick layer of mayo on both halves of the rolls, top with the gherkins, parsley, rocket and finally the fish fillets. Top with the pickled eschalots, some of the mustard seeds from the liquid and the dill. Sprinkle with sea salt, serve with lemon wedges and devour!

GIN, DILL AND LEMON ZEST-CURED SALMON

SERVES 15–20

2 bunches dill
500 g fine salt
500 g caster sugar
125 ml (½ cup) gin
10 juniper berries, lightly
    crushed
10 black peppercorns, lightly
    crushed
1 teaspoon fennel seeds
zest of 5 limes
zest of 5 lemons
1 side of salmon (about
    1.4 kg), pin-boned

Curing doesn't take as long as you would expect and it's a simple, healthy way to eat fish. Instead of just using lemon to cure the fish, this recipe uses gin to take it to the next level. The flavour has a slight suggestion of gin and tonic.

Chop three-quarters of the dill finely and combine with the salt, sugar, gin, juniper berries, peppercorns, fennel seeds, lime zest and lemon zest in a bowl.

Line a large baking tray with foil. Place 2 sheets of plastic wrap over the foil, then spread half the curing mixture over the plastic wrap. Place the salmon, skin side down, on the mixture, then top with the remaining curing mix, ensuring there is no exposed flesh. Place 2 more pieces of plastic wrap over the salmon and tightly secure them with the pieces underneath the fish. Cover with foil and place in the refrigerator to cure for 24 hours. This is a full cure, so the fish will be cured the whole way through.

Once the fish is cured, remove it from the refrigerator and rinse off the curing mixture under cold water.

Roughly chop the remaining dill and sprinkle it over the fish.

Cut across the fish to make slices as thin as possible – just before you hit the skin, turn the knife away from the skin to remove a piece. This will ensure that the fat and darker flesh next to the skin are left behind.

BRENT'S TIP: Just be careful not to overcure the fish. If it spends too much time in the curing mixture, it will turn into a stiff surfboard.

MUM'S TUNA BAKE
WITH THREE CHEESES

25 g butter
1 brown onion, finely diced
2 garlic cloves
25 g plain flour
500 ml (2 cups) milk
¼ teaspoon freshly grated
  nutmeg
80 g (½ cup) frozen peas
75 g (½ cup) frozen corn
  kernels
425 g tinned tuna in
  springwater, drained and
  flaked
460 g (2 cups) Creamy mash
  (page 24)
125 g (1 cup) grated smoked
  cheddar
50 g (½ cup) grated parmesan
75 g (½ cup) grated
  mozzarella

I ate this a lot when I was a kid - it's been in my life forever. I've added a new cheese with the smoked cheddar, but there's still the familiar parmesan and oozing, melted mozzarella.

Preheat a grill to high.

Put the butter in a large saucepan or high-sided frying pan over medium heat. Once foaming, add the onion and sweat for 5–6 minutes. Add the garlic and cook for a further 2 minutes. Add the flour and cook for 2 minutes, stirring constantly until the mixture comes together to form a paste. Slowly add the milk, whisking constantly to remove any lumps, then add the nutmeg, stirring to combine. The mixture will start to thicken after 2–3 minutes. Cook for 4–5 minutes, then add the peas, corn and tuna. Stir and cook for a further 5–7 minutes until the mixture is really thick.

Pour the mixture into a 2 litre (8 cup) capacity greased baking dish. Top the mixture with the mashed potato and scatter over the grated cheeses. Place the dish under the grill and cook until the cheese has melted and is golden brown, about 10 minutes. Alternatively, cook in a 200°C oven (or 180°C for a fan-forced oven) for 15–20 minutes or until heated through and lightly browned on top.

BRENT'S TIP: Béchamel sauce is the base for cheese sauces, the sauce in a lasagne and the base of a lot of French dishes. A velouté is almost the same but a lot lighter in consistency. The basic béchamel sauce formula is 1:10, flour + butter to milk – i.e., 25 g flour + 25 g butter = 50 g, so you'd need 500 ml milk. To make a béchamel into a velouté, simply replace half the milk with a flavoured stock.

CHICKEN BRAISED IN RED WINE
WITH MUSHROOMS

SERVES 4

2 rashers bacon, thinly sliced

2 kg chicken, jointed (see
   page 140 or ask your
   butcher to do this)

6 baby onions, skins removed
   and halved

2 garlic cloves, crushed

2 carrots, chopped into
   small chunks

1 teaspoon tomato paste

50 g unsalted butter

1 teaspoon plain flour

60 ml (¼ cup) port

750 ml (3 cups) red wine
   (shiraz)

750 ml (3 cups) chicken stock

2 bay leaves

4 thyme sprigs

200 g Swiss brown
   mushrooms, cut into cubes

large handful flat-leaf parsley,
   finely chopped

This dish is rich and delicious and a perfect winter warmer. There's also sweetness from the port but the pickled onions cut through the richness. Serve it with Creamy mash (page 24), vegetable purée (see page 13), polenta or crusty bread.

Put the bacon in a flameproof casserole dish, then set over high heat. As the dish heats up, the fat will be released from the bacon. Continue to cook until caramelised, about 5–6 minutes. Remove the bacon from the dish, reserving the oil in the dish. Set the bacon aside. Add the chicken pieces and sear on all sides until golden. Remove the chicken from the dish and transfer to a plate.

Reduce the heat to medium, add the onions and sweat for about 4–5 minutes. Add the garlic and carrot and cook for 2–3 minutes. Add the tomato paste, 20 g of the butter and the flour and cook for 2 minutes, stirring constantly to avoid the mixture sticking to the dish. Increase the heat to high then add the port and cook for 2 minutes. Add the red wine and stock and bring to the boil. Add the bay leaves and 3 of the thyme sprigs and put the chicken in the liquid, ensuring it is completely covered. Put the lid on, reduce the heat to medium–low and cook for 1–1½ hours, or until the chicken is falling off the bone.

Put the remaining thyme sprig and the remaining butter in a small frying pan over medium heat. Once the butter is foaming, add the mushrooms and cook gently for 5–6 minutes or until tender. Spoon the mushrooms into the chicken dish. Remove the bay leaves and thyme stalks from the dish, scatter over the chopped parsley and reserved crispy bacon and serve.

FRIED CHICKEN
WITH CHIPOTLE MAYO

SERVES 4

1.8 kg chicken
3 eggs
60 ml (¼ cup) Tabasco sauce,
  plus extra to serve
2 teaspoons garlic powder
2 teaspoons onion powder
1 teaspoon salt
150 g (1 cup) self-raising flour
vegetable oil for deep-frying
Chipotle mayo (page 23)
  to serve

Fried chicken is always delicious but infusing some chilli heat and smokiness into it adds more interest. You get the tingle of the chilli on your lips and the creamy mayo drips all over your fingers – it's a fun and delicious experience. Dive in!

To joint the chicken, using a sharp knife, remove the wings and legs, separating the thighs from the drumsticks. Cut the first joint from the wings and discard. Remove the breasts from the chicken and cut each breast into 2 portions widthways. Remove the skin from the leg and breast portions. You will have 8 pieces of chicken.

In a large bowl, lightly whisk the eggs. Add 60 ml (¼ cup) water and the Tabasco, whisk together and set aside.

In a plastic bag combine the garlic and onion powders, ½ teaspoon of the salt and a good grinding of black pepper. In a separate bag combine the flour and remaining salt.

Fill a large saucepan one-third full with vegetable oil and place it over medium heat for the oil to heat up.

Pat the chicken dry with paper towel and place the breast pieces in the plastic bag with the garlic and onion powders. Shake well then remove the chicken pieces and place them in the egg mixture. Coat them well with the egg and then put them in the bag with the flour. Shake well again. Repeat with the other pieces of chicken.

Check that the oil is at the right temperature by dipping a wooden spoon handle in the oil. If the oil bubbles around the handle, it's hot enough. Place the chicken legs and wings in the oil, ensuring you don't overcrowd the pan. Turn the chicken over after 6 minutes and cook for a further 6–8 minutes, or until deep golden and cooked through. Transfer to paper towel to absorb any excess oil. Repeat with the chicken breast, cooking for 8–10 minutes (the breast pieces will take less time to cook). Serve with the chipotle mayo and some extra Tabasco sauce if you want a bit of extra kick.

CHICKEN PARMIGIANA
WITH CHEDDAR AND ALE

SERVES 4

250 ml (1 cup) dark ale beer
375 g (1⅓ cups) Smoked
    tomato relish (page 32)
vegetable oil for deep-frying
4 chicken breast fillets (600 g
    in total), butterflied
75 g (½ cup) plain flour
2 eggs, lightly whisked
120 g (2 cups) panko crumbs
large handful chopped
    flat-leaf parsley
4 slices prosciutto
250 g (2 cups) grated cheddar
75 g (½ cup) grated
    mozzarella
Celeriac and apple slaw
    (page 112) to serve

A lot of my mates go to the pub and have a chicken parma. So why not incorporate beer in the sauce! Serve this with the slaw or Perfect chips (page 24).

Cook the beer and tomato relish in a small saucepan over high heat until reduced, thick and sticky, about 5–7 minutes. Remove the pan from the heat and set aside.

Fill a deep-fryer or large saucepan one-third full with vegetable oil and set over medium heat. Heat the oil to 180°C.

Using a rolling pin, lightly bash the chicken breasts so they are an even size, about 1 cm thick.

Put the flour in one bowl, the whisked egg in a second bowl and the panko crumbs and parsley in a third bowl. Dip the chicken in the flour, then the egg and finally the panko crumbs.

Check the temperature of the oil by dipping a wooden spoon handle in the oil – if the oil bubbles around the handle, then it's hot enough. Add the chicken in batches and deep-fry for 6–8 minutes or until golden brown. Remove and immediately transfer to paper towel to absorb any excess oil.

Cook the prosciutto in a dry frying pan over high heat until crispy, about 30–60 seconds each side. Cool, then cut into strips.

Combine the cheeses and cooled prosciutto strips. Top the chicken breasts with the smoked tomato relish and ale mixture and then the grated cheese mixture. Cook under a hot grill until the cheese has melted and browned on top. Serve with the slaw.

THAI GREEN CHICKEN CURRY

1 tablespoon peanut oil

1 brown onion, cut into wedges

150 g small Thai green eggplants, trimmed and halved

60 g (¼ cup) Thai green curry paste (page 30)

270 ml coconut cream

60 ml (¼ cup) chicken stock

1 tablespoon shaved palm sugar

2 tablespoons fish sauce

juice of 1 lime

600 g chicken thigh fillets, cut into 4 pieces

small handful snow peas

1 long green chilli, thinly sliced, to serve

4 kaffir lime leaves, finely shredded

bunch fresh coriander leaves to serve

steamed rice to serve

Green chicken curry is one of my favourite dishes as it contains those awesome Southeast Asian flavours of lime, ginger, garlic and fish sauce. I often ramp up the lime and ginger as I can't get enough of them!

Heat the peanut oil in a large wok over high heat. When hot, add the onion and eggplant and cook, stirring constantly, for 2–3 minutes, until the vegetables are just tender.

Reduce the heat to medium, add the curry paste and cook, stirring constantly, for a further 2 minutes, or until the paste releases its aroma. Add the coconut cream and stock and stir until well combined.

Allow to come to a simmer, stirring occasionally, then add the palm sugar, fish sauce, lime juice and chicken. Bring to a simmer again then reduce the heat to medium–low and cook for 8–10 minutes, until the chicken is almost cooked through, stirring every couple of minutes. Add the snow peas and cook for a further 2 minutes.

Taste for seasoning then serve topped with the chilli, kaffir lime leaves and coriander. Serve with simple steamed rice.

BRENT'S TIP: If you can't find Thai eggplants, use a small sliced zucchini instead. Add it when you add the snow peas.

MUM'S CHICKEN CACCIATORE

SERVES 4

4 slices pancetta, thinly sliced
   into strips
2 tablespoons olive oil
2 kg chicken, jointed (see
   page 140 or you can ask
   your butcher to do this
   for you)
4 baby onions, quartered
4 garlic cloves, crushed
5 anchovy fillets in oil, drained
   and roughly chopped
1 tablespoon tomato paste
60 ml (¼ cup) white wine
   vinegar
1 tablespoon brown sugar
700 ml tomato passata
125 ml (½ cup) chicken stock
70 g (½ cup) black olives,
   freshly pitted
vegetable oil for deep-frying
large handful flat-leaf
   parsley leaves
50 g (¼ cup) capers

Mum used to cook this when I was young, but it was a much simpler dish. I've added the classic Italian flavours of anchovies, pancetta, olives and capers to take it to the next level. This would be great with warm crusty bread or served on a bed of creamy polenta.

Place a large flameproof casserole over high heat. Add the pancetta and cook until crispy, about 2–3 minutes. Remove the pancetta from the pan and add the olive oil.

Season the chicken, add it to the pan and brown it on all sides in the oil. Remove the chicken from the pan and transfer to a plate. Reduce the heat to medium and add the baby onions, garlic and anchovies and cook for 2 minutes, scraping the bottom of the pan. Add the tomato paste and cook for a further 2 minutes. Add the white wine vinegar and cook until the liquid has reduced by half, about 5 minutes. Add the brown sugar, passata and stock and return the chicken to the pan. Stir, cover and cook over low heat for 1½ hours or until the chicken is falling off the bone. If the sauce is still watery, cook for a further 15 minutes with the lid removed. Add the pitted olives and stir to combine. Check for seasoning.

While the stew is cooking, fill a medium saucepan one-third full with vegetable oil and set over high heat. Check if the oil is hot enough by placing a wooden spoon handle into the oil. If the oil bubbles around the spoon, it's ready. Throw in half the parsley leaves, but stand back because it will spit. Cook for 30 seconds then transfer to paper towel to absorb any excess oil. Repeat with half the capers but cook for 2–3 minutes.

When the chicken is cooked, transfer it to a large bowl, drizzle over the sauce, top with the remaining fresh parsley and fresh capers as well as the fried parsley and capers. Serve hot.

CHILLI CON CARNE

SERVES 6

1 kg beef chuck steak,
   trimmed of sinew, cut into
   5 cm chunks
35 g (¼ cup) plain flour
½ teaspoon salt
2 tablespoons olive oil
2 brown onions, finely diced
3 garlic cloves, crushed
1 green capsicum, diced
2 teaspoons dried chilli flakes
1 teaspoon ground cumin
½ teaspoon ground coriander
½ teaspoon dried oregano
½ teaspoon cayenne pepper
½ teaspoon cocoa powder
1 tablespoon tomato paste
400 g tinned diced tomatoes
1 litre (4 cups) beef stock
400 g tinned red kidney
   beans, drained and rinsed
fresh coriander leaves
   to serve

This is a pretty classic chilli con carne and it's not too hot. I have used cubes of beef instead of the more usual mince and then the meat is shredded at the end. You could put a sheet of pastry over the top and bake this into a pie. Or try it on a baked potato, in a quesadilla or with Mexican barbecued corn salad (page 112) and rice.

Place the beef in a large clean plastic bag. Add the flour and salt, twist the top of the bag and give it a good shake until the meat is well coated with the flour mixture.

Set a flameproof casserole over high heat. Add the oil and wait until it is very hot. Add a batch of the chuck steak, without overcrowding the pan, and brown on all sides. Transfer to a plate and repeat until all the beef has been browned. Set the meat aside.

Reduce the heat to medium and add the onion, garlic and capsicum to the pan and sweat for 4–5 minutes. Add the chilli flakes, cumin, coriander, oregano, cayenne pepper and cocoa powder and give it a good stir. If the pan is drying out, add 60 ml (¼ cup) water and continue cooking. Cook for a further 2 minutes then add the tomato paste. Cook for 2 minutes then add the tinned tomatoes and beef stock and return the steak to the pan. Bring to the boil then cover and cook for 1½ hours over medium–low heat. After 1 hour remove the lid and turn the heat up to medium to reduce the liquid.

Add the kidney beans and heat through for 5 minutes. Check for seasoning and adjust if necessary.

When the meat is cooked and tender, gently tear it apart in the pan using 2 forks. Transfer to a serving bowl and garnish with the fresh coriander.

BEEF CHEEKS
BRAISED WITH CHOCOLATE

SERVES 4

2 tablespoons olive oil
4 beef cheeks (about 1.6 kg in total), sinew trimmed
2 large brown onions, cut into wedges
3 garlic cloves, thinly sliced
4 carrots, cut into small chunks
125 ml (½ cup) red wine vinegar
125 ml (½ cup) port
1.25 litres (5 cups) beef stock
200 g green beans, trimmed
1 square dark chocolate (at least 70% cocoa solids)

CAULIFLOWER PURÉE
30 g butter
2 eschalots (French shallots), thinly sliced
2 garlic cloves, thinly sliced
1 cauliflower, very thinly sliced
60 ml (¼ cup) vegetable stock
2 tablespoons pouring cream

The slow-cooked beef cheeks are rich and melt in your mouth. Serve them on a bed of the cauliflower purée with the green beans on the side. The cooking time can vary a lot, so check your meat every 30 minutes. You want the meat to be shreddable, but still holding its shape.

Preheat the oven to 190°C (or 170°C for a fan-forced oven).

Heat the olive oil in a deep flameproof casserole over high heat. Season the beef cheeks with salt and pepper, add them to the pan in batches and cook until golden on both sides, about 5–6 minutes. Remove the meat from the pan and transfer to a plate. Reduce the heat to medium, add the onion and cook for 4–5 minutes. Add the garlic and carrots and cook for a further 2–3 minutes. Increase the heat to high again, add the vinegar and cook for 2–3 minutes, then add the port. Cook to reduce the liquid for a further 2–3 minutes, return the beef cheeks to the pan and add enough beef stock to cover. Bring to the boil, cover and transfer to the oven. Cook for 2½–4 hours or until the cheeks are able to be pulled apart with a fork, but still hold their shape.

Meanwhile, for the cauliflower purée, melt the butter in a medium saucepan over medium–high heat. Add the eschalots and sweat for 2 minutes. Add the garlic and sweat for a further minute. Add the cauliflower and vegetable stock, stir and cover, then cook for 10–12 minutes or until very tender. Remove the pan from the heat, add the cream and blitz with a hand-held blender until you have a fine purée. Check for seasoning and set aside.

Steam the beans over a large saucepan of simmering water or until just tender. Remove the beef from the pan and strain the liquid into another saucepan over high heat. Reserve the carrots from the sieve. Reduce the liquid until slightly thickened, for about 15 minutes, then stir in the chocolate until melted and season with salt. Return the carrots to the sauce. Dip the cheeks in the sauce before serving with the beans and cauliflower purée (and the carrots if you like).

SLOW-ROASTED LAMB SHOULDER
WITH HARISSA

SERVES 6

---

2 kg lamb shoulder, bone in
lemon wedges to serve
mint leaves to serve

HARISSA
10 long red chillies, roughly
    chopped
3 garlic cloves, peeled
1 teaspoon ground cumin
½ teaspoon ground caraway
1 teaspoon ground coriander
½ teaspoon salt
2 tablespoons olive oil

MINT AND YOGHURT DIP
juice of ½ lemon
handful chopped mint
250 g (1 cup) natural Greek-
    style yoghurt

This is my take on the Aussie classic, roast lamb. I've added interest by slow-cooking and then shredding the meat, and serving it with a spicy harissa. There is also a cooling mint and yoghurt dip for freshness. Serve with flatbreads.

Preheat the oven to 180°C (or 160°C for a fan-forced oven).

For the harissa, put the chillies, garlic, spices, salt and olive oil in a blender or food processor and blitz to form a fine paste, adding a little water to help it mix, if required. Spread the harissa over the lamb and set aside to marinate for at least 1 hour.

Put 750 ml (3 cups) water in a large roasting tin. Put in a roasting rack and place the lamb on top. Cover the lamb with foil and roast in the oven for 2 hours. After 2 hours, remove the foil and roast for a further 2 hours, or until the lamb can be pulled apart with 2 forks but still holds its shape.

For the dip, combine all the ingredients in a small bowl.

Serve the lamb with the yoghurt dip, lemon wedges and mint leaves.

SPICY BEEF AND PORK MEATLOAF

SERVES 4–6

2 tablespoons worcestershire
    sauce
1 tablespoon wholegrain
    mustard
1 teaspoon hot English
    mustard
125 ml (½ cup) tomato sauce
1 tablespoon brown sugar
500 g beef mince
250 g pork mince
1 egg, lightly beaten
½ brown onion, grated
1 small zucchini, grated
1 small carrot, grated
100 g (1 cup) dry breadcrumbs
Creamy mash (page 24)
    to serve

This updated spicy meatloaf is delicious served with mashed potatoes and greens or roast vegetables. The leftovers are also great in sandwiches the next day.

Preheat the oven to 200°C (or 180°C for a fan-forced oven).

Line 4 individual 300 ml loaf tins or a 1.2 litre loaf tin with baking paper, extending the paper up over the long sides.

Combine the worcestershire sauce, mustards, tomato sauce and sugar in a bowl and mix together with a whisk. Set aside.

In a large bowl combine the beef, pork, egg, onion, zucchini, carrot and breadcrumbs. Season with salt and pepper, then divide the mixture into 4 or form the mixture into a large log shape.

Push the meat mixture into the loaf tin/s, pushing down to remove any air bubbles. Pour over the mustard mixture and bake the individual loaves for 30–35 minutes, or the large loaf for 55–60 minutes, or until firm to the touch. Serve with the mash.

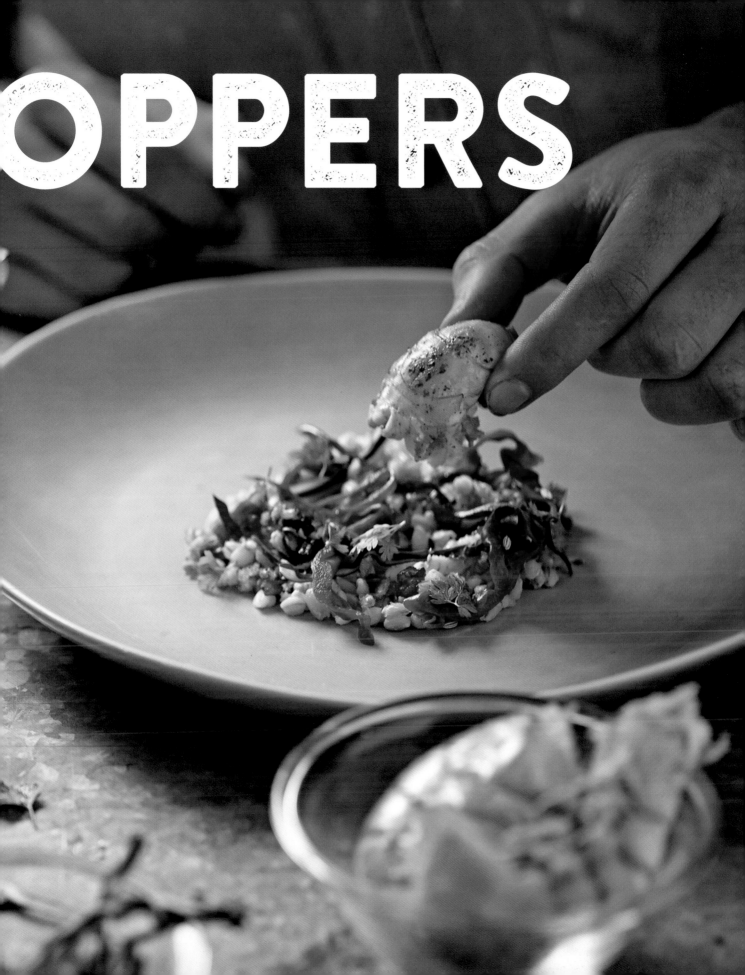

OPPERS

The recipes in this chapter are a combination of some that won me challenges on *MasterChef* or that I did well with, but others are just my own favourites – things I think are interesting and show my development. The majority are exactly as I cooked them on the show, but I've tweaked a few here and there.

These recipes are quite sophisticated and represent the high end of my cooking style now, but I don't always cook like this. The techniques that I learned have become part of the mix and I incorporate them with my more usual rustic style. I know I can cook like this when I need to, and how to think when I'm reinventing or creating dishes, but I generally go back to hearty, homestyle food every time.

Don't be fazed by the recipes in this chapter. Some of the dishes might look like complicated fine dining, but they are all achievable.

LOBSTER BISQUE
WITH CORIANDER OIL

4 small uncooked lobsters/
  crayfish
2 bunches coriander
125 ml (½ cup) olive oil
4 carrots, roughly chopped
5 tomatoes, 4 roughly
  chopped and 1 thinly sliced
400 ml white port
80 ml (⅓ cup) white vinegar
500 ml (2 cups) pouring cream
40 g butter

This is a classic French dish, but I've added some coriander oil for freshness. You can serve this as a regular soup in a bowl, but why not try it as a shooter in a small cup or glass with a little bit of cooked yabby or lobster?

Preheat the oven to 200°C (or 180°C for a fan-forced oven).

Put the lobsters in the freezer 30 minutes before using, to put them to sleep in the most humane way possible.

Bring a large saucepan of water to the boil over high heat. Add half the coriander and blanch for 30 seconds. Transfer to an ice bath.

Add the lobsters to the boiling water and blanch for 2 minutes. Transfer the lobsters to an ice bath, then remove the tails, cut them in half lengthways and set aside. Chop the heads and bodies into 2 cm pieces.

Put the chopped lobster pieces (not the tails) on a baking tray and roast in the oven for 20 minutes.

Reduce the oven to 100°C (or 80°C for a fan-forced oven).

Put 2 tablespoons of the oil in a large saucepan over medium–high heat, add the carrot, roughly chopped tomatoes and remaining coriander and fry until golden and soft, about 5–7 minutes. Add the roasted lobster pieces and cook for a further 5 minutes.

Add the port and vinegar and cook until the liquid has reduced by half, about 8–10 minutes. Add 500 ml (2 cups) water and allow to simmer until all the liquid has reduced to 150 ml, about 25 minutes. Strain into a clean saucepan and set aside. Discard the solids.

Place the tomato slices on a baking tray lined with baking paper and roast in the oven for about 30 minutes until the tomatoes are semi-dried.

To make the coriander oil, remove the blanched coriander from the ice bath and squeeze it dry. Transfer to a food processor with the remaining olive oil and blitz until well combined. Let sit for 10 minutes then strain through a fine sieve. Set aside.

Return the saucepan with the reduced stock to a low heat, add the cream and stir until combined. Once hot, remove from the heat, set aside and keep warm.

Place the butter in a frying pan over low heat. Once the butter has melted, add the lobster tail halves and fry them, basting with the butter, until just cooked, about 2 minutes per side.

Transfer the lobster to serving bowls and pour over the bisque. Top with the tomato slices, drizzle with the coriander oil, season with salt and pepper and serve.

HOMEMADE CHEESE, PICKLED PEAR, BEETROOT
AND CONFIT FENNEL SALAD

30 g (¼ cup) walnuts
420 ml grapeseed oil
2 small (about 350 g each)
   bulbs fennel, 1 cut into
   wedges and 1 thinly sliced,
   fronds reserved
2 medium beetroot, 1 kept
   whole, 1 halved with 1 of
   these halves thinly sliced
150 g rock salt
175 ml (½ cup) honey
30 ml apple cider vinegar
1 tablespoon pouring cream
20 g butter

FRESH CHEESE
2 litres (8 cups) milk
30 ml apple cider vinegar

PICKLED PEAR
140 ml apple cider vinegar
2 tablespoons sugar
1 pear

Chances are you will have most of the ingredients for this in your kitchen cupboard or fridge. The salad uses just a few ingredients in a few different ways to create something special. Cooking fennel this way makes it the hero of the dish, rather than just being a filler. Roasted and fresh beetroot are added for both interest and a pop of colour. For this dish you will make your own fresh cheese or 'panir', but it's simple.

Preheat the oven to 200°C (or 180°C for a fan-forced oven).

Put the walnuts on a baking tray lined with baking paper and toast in the oven for 3–5 minutes, or until fragrant. Set aside and allow to cool.

To make the cheese, place the milk in a large saucepan over high heat and bring to the boil, stirring occasionally. Add the vinegar and stir until the milk splits.

Remove the pan from the heat and pour the mixture into a muslin-lined sieve and strain, reserving the solids and discarding the liquid. Drain for 15–20 minutes until the mixture is quite thick.

Wrap the solids in the muslin and squeeze them gently to form a log shape, about 12 cm long. Twist the ends to secure them and set aside in the refrigerator.

For the pickled pear, thinly slice the pear lengthways until reaching the core, then slice from the other side.

Put the vinegar and sugar in a saucepan over medium heat and bring to the boil. Remove the pan from the heat, add the pear slices and set aside to pickle for 30 minutes.

Place 400 ml of the grapeseed oil in a small saucepan over low heat. Heat to 100°C, then add the fennel wedges and cook very gently, keeping the oil at 100°C, until the fennel is soft, about 45 minutes. Drain and set aside.

Wrap the whole and unsliced half beetroot in foil and place on top of the rock salt on a baking tray. Roast in the oven until tender, about 40 minutes. Remove from the oven, unwrap and cut the beetroot into small cubes. Reserve 1 tablespoon of the salt. Set the beetroot aside.

Place the honey in a small saucepan over low heat. Add the uncooked fennel slices and simmer gently until tender, about 20 minutes. Remove the fennel and set aside. Add the vinegar, cream, butter and salt and pepper to taste and whisk to combine. Allow to simmer until reduced by half, about 8 minutes. Remove from the heat and set aside.

Place the toasted walnuts and the left-over rock salt in a mortar and pestle and crush to a coarse powder.

Slice the reserved cheese into slices. Heat the remaining grapeseed oil in a non-stick frying pan over medium heat. Add the cheese slices and fry them until golden, about 1 minute on each side.

To serve, divide the pickled pear, sliced fresh beetroot, roasted beetroot, fennel wedges and slices and the cheese between the serving plates. Drizzle with the honey–cream sauce and season with salt and pepper to taste. Top with the reserved fennel fronds and sprinkle with the walnut powder.

HOMEMADE CHEESE,
PICKLED PEAR, BEETROOT
AND CONFIT FENNEL SALAD

WALNUT-CRUSTED SARDINES
WITH CURDS AND WHEY

125 g (1 cup) walnuts

125 ml (½ cup) milk

125 ml (½ cup) natural yoghurt

450 g sweet potato, cut into thin discs using a mandoline

1 tablespoon goji berries, rehydrated in hot water for 10–15 minutes until tender, drained

3 leaves Tuscan kale (cavolo nero), leaves and stems separated

60 ml (¼ cup) olive oil

2 eggs

35 g (¼ cup) wholemeal flour

8 sardines, heads and spines removed, butterflied

This dish is a bunch of healthy ingredients made delicious and was created for a superfood challenge on *MasterChef*. You make your own labna, which is a kind of yoghurt cheese and you use the left-over whey to cook the sweet potato for extra flavour and goodness. The rehydrated goji berries are like blueberries in texture and give a great flavour pop. The sardines are coated in a crunchy walnut crumb.

Preheat the oven to 200°C (or 180°C for a fan-forced oven).

Put the walnuts on a baking tray lined with baking paper and toast in the oven for 3–5 minutes, or until fragrant. Set aside and allow to cool. Transfer to a food processor and blitz until you have a coarse crumb consistency.

Put the milk in a saucepan over medium heat. Once the milk begins to simmer, add the yoghurt and stir gently until the liquid splits and curds form. Remove from the heat and strain the whey (liquid) through a muslin-lined sieve into a clean saucepan, reserving the curds.

Place the saucepan of whey over medium heat, add two-thirds of the sweet potato discs and simmer, covered, until the sweet potato is soft, about 12–15 minutes.

Remove from the heat, drain and pass through a sieve or purée with a hand-held blender. Add the softened goji berries and stir to combine, season with salt and pepper and set aside.

Place the 3 kale stems on a baking tray and cook in the oven until completely black, about 20 minutes. Allow to cool then crush and pass through a sieve to make a dust. Set aside.

Place the remaining sweet potato discs on a baking tray lined with baking paper and cook in the oven until lightly browned and crisp, 10–15 minutes, turning halfway through cooking time. Remove from the oven and set aside.

Reduce the oven to 180°C (or 160°C for a fan-forced oven).

Tear the kale leaves into pieces and rub them all over with ½ teaspoon of the olive oil. Place on another lined baking tray and cook for 12–15 minutes or until crisp.

Crack the eggs into a small bowl and lightly whisk them.

Put the crushed walnuts and flour in a small bowl and stir to combine.

Dip the sardines first in the egg and then in the nut mixture and then repeat to form a double coating.

Fry the sardines in the remaining oil in a frying pan over medium heat, until golden and cooked through, about 1–2 minutes per side.

Place the sardines on serving plates with some sweet potato purée, roasted sweet potato discs, the curds and kale crisps. Sprinkle with the kale dust, season and serve.

THAI RED PRAWNS

WITH COCONUT– LEMONGRASS PANNA COTTA

2 mango cheeks, cut into
   1 cm strips
12 raw king prawns, peeled
   and deveined, tails intact
80 ml (⅓ cup) peanut oil
2 teaspoons grated palm
   sugar
2 tablespoons lime juice
1 tomato, quartered, seeds
   removed and sliced into
   fine slivers
coriander leaves for garnish
roasted cashew nuts for
   garnish
thinly sliced spring onion
   for garnish
lime cheeks for garnish

Thai food is normally served in big portions for sharing, but this dish is presented in a more modern and elegant way. The red curry prawns are served with a savoury panna cotta containing the classic Thai flavours of coconut milk and lemongrass. It is the perfect accompaniment to the spicy curry.

For the panna cotta, place the coconut milk and lemongrass in a saucepan over medium heat. Bring to the boil then remove the pan from the heat. Squeeze the water from the gelatine then add the gelatine to the pan. Stir until dissolved then allow to sit to infuse for 10 minutes. Lightly spray an 18 x 28 cm tray with cooking spray. Strain the panna cotta into the prepared tray and place in the refrigerator until set, 1½–2 hours.

For the curry paste, place all the ingredients in a small food processor or blender and blitz to a fine paste. Set aside.

Place a chargrill pan over high heat. Once hot, place the mango strips on the grill and cook on both sides until grill marks appear. Remove the mango from the grill and set aside.

COCONUT–LEMONGRASS PANNA COTTA

400 ml coconut milk
1 lemongrass stem, finely chopped
5 g (2 sheets) gold-strength gelatine sheets, softened in iced water

CURRY PASTE

8 cm piece ginger, peeled and roughly chopped
2 long red chillies, roughly chopped
1 garlic clove, roughly chopped
1 tablespoon fish sauce
8 coriander stems, roughly chopped

Meanwhile, toss the prawns in 1 tablespoon of the curry paste and mix well.

Heat 1 tablespoon of the peanut oil in a large non-stick frying pan over medium–high heat and cook the prawns until just cooked through, 3–4 minutes. Remove the prawns from the pan and set aside, covered, to keep warm.

Reduce the heat to medium. Add the remaining curry paste to the pan and cook, stirring, until fragrant, about 2–3 minutes. Slowly add the remaining oil, whisking to combine. Pour into a heatproof bowl, add the palm sugar and lime juice and whisk to emulsify.

Remove the panna cotta from the refrigerator, loosen the edges and turn it carefully onto a sheet of baking paper. Slice it into four 7 x 18 cm rectangles and gently transfer to serving plates. Add the prawns, mango and tomato slivers. Drizzle with the curry paste mixture. Garnish with the coriander leaves, cashew nuts, spring onion and lime cheeks.

THAI RED PRAWNS WITH
COCONUT–LEMONGRASS
PANNA COTTA

SCAMPI WITH PICKLED CABBAGE
AND TEXTURES OF BARLEY

110 g (½ cup) pearl barley
8 scampi, shelled, with shells
  and roe reserved
1 small (about 1 kg) red
  cabbage
125 ml (½ cup) apple cider
  vinegar
110 g (½ cup) sugar
grapeseed oil for deep-frying
3 garlic cloves, thinly sliced
4 anchovy fillets, thinly sliced
2 tablespoons apera (sherry)
1 tablespoon fennel seeds
40 g butter
chervil for garnish

For this dish I tried to get the most out of barley, which is normally boiled. I decided to make three different textures – soft, chewy and crunchy. The pickled cabbage adds a lovely acidity and red cabbage juice is used to cook the scampi. You have to be careful with this dish because the scampi are so delicate that they're easily lost when using a lot of flavours, so the proportions are important. Always remember to taste everything as you go.

Preheat the oven to 200°C (or 180°C for a fan-forced oven).

Cook the barley in boiling water until tender, about 35 minutes. Remove from the heat, drain well and divide into 2 portions.

Place the reserved scampi shells on a baking tray and roast them in the oven until golden, about 20 minutes. Remove from the oven and set aside.

Thinly slice a quarter of the cabbage and set aside.

Juice the remaining cabbage and set aside – you will need about 190 ml (¾ cup) cabbage juice.

Meanwhile, to make the pickled cabbage, place the vinegar, sugar and 60 ml (¼ cup) water in a saucepan over high heat and bring to the boil. Place the thinly sliced cabbage in a heatproof bowl and pour over the boiling liquid. Set aside, stirring occasionally, for about 30 minutes.

Place 1 tablespoon of the oil in a frying pan over medium heat. Fry the garlic and anchovies, stirring frequently, for 2–3 minutes. Add the roasted scampi shells and cook for a further minute. Add

the apera and deglaze the pan. Add the cabbage juice and allow
to simmer until the liquid has reduced by half and thickened slightly,
about 6–8 minutes.

Remove the pan from the heat and strain, reserving the liquid.
Discard the solids. Add the fennel seeds to the liquid, season with
salt and pepper and set aside, keeping warm.

Fill a medium saucepan one-third full with grapeseed oil and set
over high heat. When the oil reaches 180°C or when the oil bubbles
around the handle of a wooden spoon inserted in the oil, add half
the cooked barley and deep-fry it until golden and crisp on the
outside, about 2–3 minutes. Remove the barley from the oil with
a slotted spoon and set aside on paper towel to drain.

Place the butter in a frying pan over low heat. Add the scampi
and fry it, basting well with the butter, until cooked through, about
1 minute.

To serve, spoon some boiled barley and some deep-fried barley
onto each serving plate. Top with the scampi and pickled cabbage.
Drizzle with the sauce and garnish with the chervil and scampi roe.

BRENT'S TIP: Store any left-over cabbage juice in the refrigerator.
Add it to sauces for a unique colour or add to fresh fruit juices.

SCAMPI WITH PICKLED
CABBAGE AND
TEXTURES OF BARLEY

PAN-FRIED SWORDFISH
WITH MINTED PEA AND LEMON SALAD

SERVES 4

120 g butter
500 g jerusalem artichoke,
   peeled and thinly sliced
200 g sugar snap peas
80 ml (⅓ cup) pouring cream
20 g (1 cup) mint leaves, plus
   extra for garnish
100 ml grapeseed oil
2 lemons
4 x 180 g swordfish fillets

For this dish I use sugar snap peas both in the purée and also thinly sliced in the salad. Jerusalem artichoke is a lovely creamy vegetable and makes a great purée - it makes great chips too as it has a high starch content. You don't have to use swordfish - you can use pretty much any white fish.

Place 100 g of the butter in a saucepan over medium heat. Add the artichoke slices and about two-thirds of the peas and cook, stirring occasionally, until soft, about 10–12 minutes.

Transfer the mixture to a food processor, add the cream, season with salt and pepper and blitz to a smooth purée. Pass through a sieve into a clean saucepan and set aside.

Bring a saucepan of water to the boil over high heat. Add the mint leaves and blanch them until bright green. Transfer to an ice bath.

Once cool, transfer the mint to a small food processor or blender and process, while slowly adding 75 ml of the oil, until you have a fine purée. Pass the mixture through a sieve into a clean bowl.

Squeeze the juice of 1 lemon into the mint oil and whisk until combined. Set aside.

Peel the remaining lemon and cut it into segments. Cut each segment into thirds and place them in a bowl. Thinly slice the remaining sugar snap peas lengthways and add them to the lemon segments. Set aside.

Place the remaining butter and oil in a frying pan over medium heat. Season the swordfish with salt and pepper and fry until just cooked through, about 2–3 minutes on each side.

To serve, place some jerusalem artichoke and pea purée on a serving plate and add the fish. Dot with the mint oil, add the pea and lemon salad and garnish with the extra mint leaves.

PAN-FRIED SWORDFISH WITH
MINTED PEA AND LEMON SALAD

'LIGHT AT THE END OF THE TUNNEL'

SERVES 4

½ bunch flat-leaf parsley,
   rinsed
½ bunch dill, rinsed
¼ bunch tarragon leaves,
   rinsed
½ bunch basil leaves, rinsed
handful fennel fronds, rinsed
1 tablespoon white balsamic
   vinegar
2 tablespoons mascarpone
juice of 1 lemon
125 ml (½ cup) grapeseed oil
3 x 4 g sachets squid ink
vegetable oil for deep-frying
   plus 1 additional tablespoon
8 raw prawns, peeled and
   deveined, legs reserved
12 sorrel leaves

SCALLOP BALL
48 scallops, no roe
60 g (¼ cup) sour cream
zest of 1 lemon

I created this dish for my dad, so it has huge meaning for me. It has actually developed our personal relationship since I first made it and it has brought us closer. The title of the dish is self-explanatory, really. There is a positive white scallop ball surrounded by darkness. But the pop of white is the focus and the first thing you see among the dark and it's the positive that matters. This dish is all about contrasts and it might look fancy, but it's achievable by any cook.

To make the scallop ball, slice 40 of the scallops evenly in half horizontally to make 80 discs. Place the halved scallops in a single layer between 2 sheets of plastic wrap. Using a rolling pin, very gently roll out the scallops so they are all an even size.

Chop the remaining scallops very finely. Put the chopped scallops in a bowl with the sour cream and the lemon zest and season with salt.

Tear off a 30 cm square of plastic wrap. Place the wrap lightly over a coffee cup and push it down about 6 cm in the centre to form a semi-circle shape. Line the plastic wrap with the scallop discs, slightly overlapping them in 2 concentric circles. Reserve 1 piece as a lid. Spoon in a quarter of the chopped scallop and sour cream mixture, then top with the lid, ensuring the lid will be overlapped by the outside scallops. Repeat with the remaining scallops and scallop mixture. Bring in the sides of the plastic wrap and wrap the scallops tightly to form a ball. The finished ball will be about the size of a small apple. Tie the end of the plastic wrap and place the scallop ball in the refrigerator to firm up.

Put the parsley, dill, tarragon, basil, fennel fronds, white balsamic, mascarpone and lemon juice in a large food processor. Blitz to make a fine paste. With the processor running, slowly add the grapeseed oil and continue to blitz for a few minutes. Pass the mixture through a fine sieve, discarding the pulp. Return the emulsion to the processor, add the squid ink and blitz again until fully incorporated and the mixture is black. Season to taste.

Fill a small saucepan one-third full with vegetable oil and set it over high heat. Check the temperature of the oil by dipping in the handle of a wooden spoon – if the oil bubbles around the handle, then it's hot enough. Add the prawn legs and deep-fry them for 2 minutes. Transfer to paper towel to absorb any excess oil.

Put 250 ml (1 cup) water in a small saucepan over high heat. Once boiling, add the sorrel leaves. Boil for 50 seconds then remove and plunge into iced water.

Season the prawns and put them in a small frying pan over low heat with 1 tablespoon of vegetable oil. Gently cook the prawns for 1 minute on each side until just cooked through. Remove them from the pan and transfer to paper towel to absorb any excess oil. Dip the prawns and sorrel in the black herb emulsion until well coated.

To assemble the dish, remove the scallop ball from the refrigerator and cut the knot of the plastic wrap to remove the scallop ball. Place it in the centre of a plate. Slice the prawns and sorrel leaves in half and gently place them around the scallop ball. Insert the prawn legs into the gaps and serve.

BRENT'S TIP: Try very hard not to get the squid ink onto the scallop ball as the colour will automatically stain the scallops.

CRISP PORK BELLY
WITH APPLE GEL, APPLE PICKLE AND CELERIAC PURÉE

SERVES 4

1 teaspoon Vegemite
500 ml (2 cups) beef stock
500 ml (2 cups) apple juice
375 ml (1½ cups) Guinness
   beer
1 garlic bulb, cloves separated
   and bruised
3 granny smith apples,
   2 halved and 1 peeled
   and cut into 1 cm dice
2 onions, quartered
1 kg pork belly, skin scored
1½ tablespoons salt
50 g (¼ cup) popcorn kernels
2 tablespoons olive oil
2 eschalots (French shallots),
   peeled and halved
40 g butter
crushed pepperberries
   for garnish (optional)
fennel seeds for garnish
nasturtiums or other edible
   flowers for garnish

This dish sounds really technical, but it's not. Pork belly takes a bit of time to cook as you have to render the fat and you want the crackling to be crunchy. Even though you render, or melt, the fat, the dish is still very rich, but the apple gel and apple pickle balance the flavour.

Preheat the oven to 170°C (or 150°C for a fan-forced oven).

For the pork, dissolve the Vegemite in a small amount of the beef stock and pour it into a deep roasting tin with the remaining beef stock, the apple juice and Guinness. Add the garlic, halved apples and onions.

Rub the pork skin with 2 teaspoons of the salt and lay the pork belly on top of the apples and onions, skin side up. Roast the pork, uncovered, until tender, about 2 hours.

Change the oven to the grill setting on high and grill the pork for a few minutes, moving the pork to a higher shelf if there is room, until the pork skin is crisp, about 5 minutes. If you don't have an oven grill, turn the oven to the highest setting and cook, uncovered, for a few minutes. Remove the pork from the oven and strain and reserve the pan juices. Set the pork aside, covered loosely with foil, to rest. Discard the garlic, apples and onions.

Meanwhile, for the apple gel, place the cider vinegar and apple juice in a saucepan over medium heat. Bring to the boil, add the agar agar and whisk to combine. Boil for a further 2–3 minutes until the agar agar has dissolved. Remove from the heat and pour the

APPLE GEL

100 ml apple cider vinegar
100 ml apple juice
1 teaspoon agar agar

APPLE PICKLE

60 ml (¼ cup) apple cider
  vinegar
1 tablespoon sugar
1 granny smith apple, peeled
  and cut into 1 cm dice

CELERIAC PURÉE

40 g butter
1 eschalot (French shallot),
  peeled and roughly
  chopped
1 garlic clove, crushed
1 celeriac, peeled and grated
125 ml (½ cup) vegetable
  stock
60 ml (¼ cup) milk

mixture into a 20 x 30 cm flat tray. Set aside in the refrigerator until set, about 20 minutes.

Remove the set gel from the refrigerator and transfer to a small food processor. Blitz until smooth, then pass through a fine sieve. Place the mixture in a piping bag fitted with a 5 mm plain nozzle and set aside in the refrigerator.

For the apple pickle, place the cider vinegar and sugar in a saucepan over medium heat and bring to the boil. Place the diced apple in a bowl. Pour the boiling liquid over the apple and set aside to pickle for at least 30 minutes.

Place the unpopped popcorn kernels in a saucepan over medium heat with 1 tablespoon oil. Cook, covered, until the kernels just begin to pop, about 2 minutes. Remove from the heat and discard (or eat!) the popped popcorn. Place the unpopped kernels in a small food processor. Add the remaining salt and blitz to a powder. Pass through a sieve to discard any large pieces. Set aside.

Place the remaining oil in a frying pan over medium heat. Add the eschalot halves, cut side down, and cook for 3–4 minutes. Add the butter, cover and cook for a further 5 minutes. Remove from the heat and set aside.

For the celeriac purée, heat the butter in a saucepan over medium heat. Add the eschalot and garlic and cook until translucent, about 5 minutes. Add the celeriac and stock and cook, covered, until tender, about 12 minutes.

Remove from the heat and transfer to a food processor or blender. Add the milk and process to a smooth purée. Season, set aside and keep warm.

Place the reserved and strained pan juices from the pork in a saucepan over high heat. Allow to boil until thickened and reduced, about 10 minutes. Taste for seasoning.

To serve, spread some celeriac purée on each serving plate. Slice the rested pork and place a slice on top of the purée. Add an eschalot half and some apple pickle, then pipe on some gel. Sprinkle with the popcorn powder and garnish with some of the diced apple, pepperberries (if using), fennel seeds and nasturtiums. Season to taste and serve.

CRISP PORK BELLY WITH APPLE GEL,
APPLE PICKLE AND CELERIAC PURÉE

ROAST LAMB
WITH CARAMELISED PUMPKIN AND MUSTARD CREAM

SERVES 4

2 x 300 g lamb backstraps

2 carrots, peeled and cut into finger-sized batons

2 tablespoons olive oil

½ butternut pumpkin, thinly sliced lengthways to give large sheets, seeds reserved

60 ml (¼ cup) red wine vinegar

55 g (¼ cup) sugar

1 eschalot (French shallot), thinly sliced

handful saltbush or baby English spinach leaves

2 teaspoons dried native thyme

100 g pancetta, chopped

200 g oxtail or fatty beef bones, chopped into pieces (you can ask your butcher to do this)

2 tablespoons pouring cream

2 tablespoons dijon mustard

50 g butter

30 g pigface shoots

2 teaspoons pepperberries, lightly crushed

Roast lamb is probably the most memorable Australian family dish, so why not use native Australian ingredients with it? Pepperberries are one of my favourite ingredients now. They look like large black peppercorns but when you crush them they are bright pink inside. They have a great flavour hit that's a little like szechuan pepper. Saltbush has a salty, slightly bitter flavour and pigface is a succulent. The oxtail is included to amplify the roast meat flavour. The pan juices are brushed onto the pumpkin and I use a blowtorch to inject the flavour straight into the vegetable.

Preheat the oven to 200°C (or 180°C for a fan-forced oven).

Roll each backstrap tightly in plastic wrap and secure to form a sausage shape. Set aside in the refrigerator.

Place the carrots on a baking tray, drizzle with 1 tablespoon of the olive oil and season with salt and pepper. Roast in the oven until golden and tender, about 30 minutes. Set aside and keep warm until ready to serve.

Place the pumpkin seeds on a small baking tray and roast in the oven for 20 minutes or until dried out.

Place the red wine vinegar and sugar in a saucepan and bring to the boil over high heat. Add the eschalot and remove the pan from the heat. Allow to pickle for 25–30 minutes. Drain and set aside.

Spread the saltbush on a baking tray lined with baking paper and bake for 4–5 minutes or until dried out.

Combine 2 dried saltbush leaves with the native thyme, half the roasted pumpkin seeds and salt to taste using a mortar and pestle and crush until fine. Pass the resulting mixture through a sieve and reserve the fine dust for serving.

Place the pancetta and oxtail or beef bones in a cold frying pan and bring up to medium heat. Spoon off the rendered fat every 5–10 minutes and reserve. Continue frying until the pancetta is crispy and brown, about 3–5 minutes. Discard the oxtail or bones. Drain the pancetta and set aside.

Whisk the cream and mustard until soft peaks form. Season and transfer to a small piping bag and set aside in the refrigerator.

Place the pumpkin on a baking tray lined with baking paper. Brush generously with the reserved pan juices. Using a blowtorch, caramelise the pumpkin on each side for 2–3 minutes. Alternatively, you can brown it under a hot grill. Set aside.

Heat a frying pan over high heat. Drizzle the lamb with the remaining oil and season. Cook for 2–3 minutes on each side until medium–rare. Add the butter and baste for 2–3 minutes until cooked to your liking. Remove from the pan, cover loosely with foil and allow to rest for 5 minutes.

To serve, place some pumpkin on each plate. Slice the lamb and stand it in one corner. Pipe the mustard cream around the lamb. Add the roasted carrot, pigface shoots, pickled eschalot and remaining dried saltbush leaves. Top with the crispy pancetta, crushed pepperberries, remaining pumpkin seeds and the saltbush dust. Season to taste and serve.

ROASTED RIB EYE
WITH BEETROOT AND PARSNIP

4 x 350 g beef rib eye steaks with bone, about 3 cm thick

100 ml olive oil

3 celery stalks, roughly chopped

2 large carrots, 1 roughly chopped

4 (about 600 g in total) beetroot, 1 roughly chopped

2 large parsnips, 1 peeled and cut into chunks

2 teaspoons coriander seeds

2 tablespoons fine rock salt

1 cinnamon stick

1 teaspoon fennel seeds

nasturtiums or other edible flowers for garnish

This is the first dish I created where I used one ingredient in different ways for interest. It's a very elegant beef and three veg! Some of the beetroot is roasted and the rest is smoked in a wok with cinnamon, coriander and fennel. The parsnip is cut into ribbons and baked until crispy.

Preheat the oven to 200°C (or 180°C for a fan-forced oven).

Trim the rib eye steaks and cut the meat from the bone. Set aside the beef and reserve the bone and trimmings for the sauce.

Using a cleaver, cut the bone into 2 cm chunks. Place a saucepan over high heat, add the trimmings and bones and cook them in 1 tablespoon of the oil until browned, about 5–6 minutes. Add the celery and the roughly chopped carrot and roughly chopped beetroot and cook until soft, about 10 minutes. Add 500 ml (2 cups) water and bring to the boil. Reduce the heat to low and allow to simmer until well reduced to a syrupy consistency, about 30 minutes. You should have about 80 ml (1/3 cup) liquid left. Remove from the heat, strain, season and set aside. Discard the solids.

Meanwhile, put the peeled and cut parsnip in a roasting tin. Peel and cut 2 of the remaining beetroot into 5 x 2 cm rectangles and also place them in the tin. Drizzle with 2 teaspoons of the olive oil and season. Sprinkle the beetroot with 1 teaspoon of the coriander seeds and roast the parsnip and beetroot until tender, about 20–25 minutes. Remove from the oven, set aside and keep warm.

Peel and grate the remaining carrot. Bring 250 ml (1 cup) water to the boil in a small saucepan, add the grated carrot and cook until tender, about 2 minutes.

Drain the carrot and transfer it to a food processor or blender. Add the roasted parsnip and 2 tablespoons olive oil and process to a smooth purée. Pass through a sieve, season and set aside.

Peel and thinly slice the remaining beetroot. Line a wok with foil. Add the rock salt, cinnamon stick, remaining teaspoon coriander seeds and the fennel seeds. Place a bamboo steamer or wire rack in the wok, cover the wok and place it over high heat. Once the salt starts smoking, add the beetroot slices, then cover and smoke for 10 minutes. Remove from the wok and set aside.

Peel the remaining parsnip and then continue to peel it into long ribbons. Spread the parsnip out on a baking tray, drizzle with 2 teaspoons of the oil, toss to combine and season. Place in the oven to bake until crisp, about 10 minutes.

Place a chargrill pan over high heat. Season the steaks with the remaining oil and salt and pepper. Sear in the pan for 2 minutes. Turn and sear for a further 30 seconds. Transfer to a baking tray and cook in the oven until medium–rare, about 6 minutes. Remove from the oven, season and set aside to rest.

To serve, slice the steak into 2cm thick slices. Spoon some of the purée on each plate and place the roasted and smoked beetroot beside it along with the steak. Add the parsnip ribbons and drizzle with sauce. Garnish with edible flowers.

BRENT'S TIP: If you don't have a cleaver hefty enough to cut the bone into pieces, ask your butcher to do this for you.

ROASTED RIB EYE WITH
BEETROOT AND PARSNIP

LANCASHIRE HOTPOT
WITH PARSNIP PURÉE AND POTATO GALETTES

SERVES 4

SERVES 4

600 g lamb backstrap,
  trimmed with fat reserved
2 rashers bacon, roughly
  chopped
2 eschalots (French shallots),
  peeled and roughly
  chopped
1 garlic clove, peeled and
  crushed
2 carrots, 1 roughly chopped
  and 1 peeled and finely
  chopped
250 ml (1 cup) Guinness beer
3 thyme sprigs
1 rosemary sprig
125 ml (½ cup) vegetable
  stock
2 tablespoons worcestershire
  sauce
60 g butter

I grew up eating lamb stew with mash over the top. This is a reinvention using the more elegant and crunchy potato galettes instead of mash, as well as creamy parsnip purée.

Place the trimmed lamb fat and bacon in a medium saucepan over high heat, and cook until dark and crisp, about 5 minutes. Reduce the heat to medium, add the eschalots and garlic and cook until translucent, about 2–3 minutes. Add the roughly chopped carrot and cook for a further 5 minutes. Add the Guinness, 2 of the thyme sprigs and the rosemary and allow to boil until reduced by half, about 10 minutes.

Remove from the heat and strain through a sieve. Discard the solids. Return the liquid to the pan, add the stock, the worcestershire sauce and the finely chopped carrot. Return the pan to the stove, bring to the boil and cook until the liquid has reduced by half, about 10–15 minutes. Add 20 g of the butter and whisk to combine. Remove from the heat, set aside and keep warm.

Meanwhile, for the parsnip purée, fry the eschalots in the butter in a saucepan over medium heat until translucent, about 5 minutes. Add the garlic, grated parsnip and stock. Cover and cook until the parsnip is tender, about 12 minutes. Remove from the heat.

60 g button mushrooms,
   sliced
60 g Swiss brown mushrooms,
   sliced
2 tablespoons pouring cream

PARSNIP PURÉE
2 eschalots (French shallots),
   chopped
40 g butter
1 garlic clove, crushed
4 parsnips, peeled and grated
125 ml (½ cup) vegetable
   stock

POTATO GALETTES
1 large desiree potato
20 g butter, melted

Transfer the parsnip mixture to a food processor and blitz to a smooth purée. Season, set aside and keep warm.

For the potato galettes, preheat the oven to 170°C (or 150°C for a fan-forced oven) and line a baking tray with baking paper.

Slice the potato as thinly and evenly as possible, using a mandoline if you have one. Using a 3 cm round cutter, cut discs from the potato slices – you will need about 15 discs for each of 4 potato galettes, so 60 in total.

On the baking tray, arrange 15 potato discs in 2 concentric circles as tightly as possible, with each slice overlapping the next by half to three-quarters. Brush with the melted butter and sprinkle with salt. Repeat with the remaining potato discs to make 4 galettes. Place another sheet of baking paper on top and then top with another baking tray to weight the potato down. Bake for 40–45 minutes or until crisp and golden. Allow to set and cool on the tray.

Place a chargrill pan over high heat. Season the lamb and place it in the hot pan and cook, turning, until the meat is charred on the outside and pink in the centre, about 3 minutes per side, or until cooked to your liking. Remove from the heat and set aside, covered loosely with foil to rest.

Place the remaining butter in a frying pan over medium heat. Add the mushrooms and remaining thyme sprig. Season and cook, stirring occasionally, until browned, about 5 minutes. Add the cream and cook until warmed, about 1 minute. Remove from the heat and set aside.

To serve, spread some parsnip purée on each serving plate. Cut the lamb into 3 cm cubes and place it on top. Add the galettes and mushrooms. Drizzle with the sauce, season with salt and pepper and serve.

'STRAWBERRIES AND CREAM'

SERVES 4

250 g strawberries, hulled
80 g (½ cup) blueberries
20 g caster sugar
2 teaspoons rosewater
35 g (⅓ cup) pistachio nuts, crushed

PANNA COTTA

5 g (2½ sheets) gold strength gelatine sheets
250 ml (1 cup) milk
250 ml (1 cup) pouring cream
1 vanilla bean, split and seeds scraped
40 g caster sugar

This dish is filled with lots of textures and contrasts and has some Middle Eastern flavours. There are two different textures of jelly, crispy toffee shards and dehydrated strawberries for sprinkling over at the end. You use agar agar for the rosewater jelly as the panna cotta sits on top and you don't want it to melt. The Champagne and strawberry sauce is a clear, delicious rose-pink syrup with an amazingly intense strawberry flavour.

Preheat the oven to 100°C (or 80°C for a fan-forced oven). Lightly spray four 125 ml (½ cup) dariole moulds with cooking spray. Line a baking tray with baking paper.

For the panna cotta, soak the gelatine sheets in cold water for 2–3 minutes.

In a small saucepan over medium heat, bring the milk, cream, split vanilla bean and seeds and sugar to the boil. Squeeze the excess liquid from the gelatine, add the gelatine to the pan and remove the pan from the heat. Stir until the gelatine has dissolved. Pass through a sieve and pour into the prepared moulds. Place in the refrigerator to set for 3–4 hours.

Thinly slice 4 of the strawberries and place them on the lined baking tray. Bake in the oven for about 45 minutes until dehydrated, turning the slices over after 30 minutes. Remove the strawberry slices from the oven and set aside.

For the Champagne and strawberry sauce, place the strawberries, sugar and Champagne in a bowl over a saucepan of water on medium–low heat. Cook, covered, stirring occasionally until softened, about 35–40 minutes. Remove the pan from the heat and pour the mixture through a sieve lined with 2 layers of muslin. Reserve the strawberry juices and discard the strawberries.

CHAMPAGNE AND STRAWBERRY SAUCE

500 g strawberries, hulled
20 g caster sugar
60 ml (¼ cup) Champagne or sparkling white wine

ROSEWATER JELLY

150 g caster sugar
1 teaspoon agar agar
2 teaspoons rosewater

TOFFEE

60 g caster sugar

For the rosewater jelly, place the sugar and 300 ml water in a saucepan over medium heat and bring to the boil. Add the agar agar and boil for 5 minutes until dissolved. Remove from the heat and pass through a fine sieve. Add the rosewater, mix well and pour into an 11 x 21 cm loaf tin, filling it to a depth of about 2 cm and refrigerate until set, about 45 minutes.

For the toffee, place the sugar and 1 tablespoon water in a small saucepan over low heat. Cook the syrup until it is light golden in colour, about 3–4 minutes. Pour it onto a sheet of baking paper and carefully lift one side of the paper so the toffee spreads out thinly. Set aside to harden.

Chop the remaining strawberries and put them in a bowl with the blueberries, sugar and rosewater. Stir and set aside to macerate until the sugar dissolves, about 15 minutes.

To serve, lightly crush half of the toffee and break the other half into shards.

Turn the rosewater jelly out of the tin and, using a round cookie cutter, cut out discs a little larger than the panna cotta bases (to allow for a little spreading of the panna cotta). Place the jelly discs in shallow serving bowls.

Remove the panna cottas from the refrigerator and unmould them onto the jelly bases.

Top with the toffee shards, scatter with the dehydrated strawberries, macerated berries, crushed toffee and pistachio nuts. Serve a jug of the Champagne and strawberry sauce on the side.

WHITE CHOCOLATE PANNA COTTA

WITH COCONUT CRUMBLE AND PASSIONFRUIT SYRUP

SERVES 4

2 coconuts
lemon segments, cut into pieces, to serve
fresh coconut slivers for garnish

WHITE CHOCOLATE
PANNA COTTA
200 ml milk
40 g caster sugar
200 g white chocolate, broken into pieces
3 g (1½ sheets) gold-strength gelatine sheets, softened in water

COCONUT JELLY
200 ml fresh coconut water
½ teaspoon agar agar

Passionfruit and white chocolate are a match made in heaven. I've also added textural contrasts to this panna cotta, with the coconut jelly and coconut crumble.

Crack open the coconuts over a large bowl (see Brent's tips) and reserve 200 ml of the coconut water for the coconut jelly. Grate about 1 cup of coconut for the coconut crumble. Slice some slivers of coconut for garnish and set aside. Save the remaining coconut for another use.

For the panna cotta, place the milk and sugar in a saucepan over medium heat and bring to the boil. Add the white chocolate then remove the pan from the heat and stir until the chocolate has melted. Squeeze the water from the softened gelatine sheets, add them to the pan and stir until dissolved. Lightly spray four 100 ml moulds with cooking spray. Strain the panna cotta mixture and pour it into the moulds. Place in the refrigerator until set, about 2–3 hours.

Preheat the oven to 180°C (or 160°C for a fan-forced oven).

To make the coconut jelly, place the coconut water in a saucepan over high heat and bring to the boil. Add the agar agar and boil for 2 minutes or until dissolved. Pour the mixture into a 9 x 19 cm loaf tin. Place in the refrigerator to set for about 1 hour.

DIG IN!

PASSIONFRUIT SYRUP
30 g caster sugar
pulp from 4 passionfruit

COCONUT CRUMBLE
90 g (1 cup) freshly grated
  coconut
80 g (⅓ cup) caster sugar
50 g hazelnuts, plus extra for
  garnish
40 g white chocolate, broken
  into pieces

To make the passionfruit syrup, place the sugar and 30 ml water in a small saucepan over medium heat. Allow to boil for 2–3 minutes until the liquid has reduced slightly, then add the passionfruit pulp and stir to combine. Remove from the heat and set aside to cool.

To make the coconut crumble, place the grated coconut on a baking tray and roast it in the oven until golden, about 10 minutes, stirring halfway through. Remove from the oven and set aside to cool. Place the sugar and 2 tablespoons water in a saucepan over medium heat. Allow to boil until the caramel is light brown, then remove from the heat and pour it over a sheet of baking paper and allow it to set. Break off and reserve 4 shards of the toffee for serving, if you like.

Dry-fry the hazelnuts in a frying pan over medium heat for about 3–4 minutes. Allow to cool then place in a clean tea towel or in paper towel and gently rub together to remove the outer papery skin.

Set aside a few hazelnuts for garnish and transfer the remaining hazelnuts to a food processor and pulse twice. Add the white chocolate and pulse twice more. Add the remaining toffee and pulse twice more. Add the cooled grated coconut and pulse twice more, or until the mixture reaches a coarse crumb-like consistency. Set aside.

To serve, unmould the panna cottas onto serving plates. Unmould the coconut jelly and cut it into 1 cm cubes. Add the jelly to the serving plates, drizzle with the passionfruit syrup, add some coconut crumble, extra hazelnuts, lemon segments, coconut slivers and toffee shards (if using).

BRENT'S TIPS: To crack the coconuts, holding the coconut over a bowl and using the back of a cleaver, hit the coconut in the centre with medium force. Rotate it 180 degrees and repeat with a little more force. This should crack the coconut open.

To use the left-over coconut, toast it in a 70°C oven, then sprinkle over your muesli for breakfast, blitz it into smoothies for a coconut hit or roll your favourite ice cream in it to add a whole new dimension.

Dip the panna cotta moulds briefly in hot water to help release them from the moulds.

WHITE CHOCOLATE PANNA COTTA
WITH COCONUT CRUMBLE AND
PASSIONFRUIT SYRUP

PISTACHIO CAKE
WITH APPLE CLOUD, FENNEL AND CINNAMON ICE CREAM

SERVES 6

CINNAMON ICE CREAM (MAKES ABOUT 500 ML)
200 ml milk
1 cinnamon stick
3 egg yolks
30 g caster sugar
200 g sour cream
liquid nitrogen for freezing
15 g freeze-dried apple, crushed

PISTACHIO CAKE
125 g (1 cup) icing sugar mixture
125 g unsalted butter, softened
110 g (¾ cup) pistachio nuts, ground
70 g (⅔ cup) ground almonds
pinch of salt
4 eggs
40 g pistachio paste

This is another dish based on textural and flavour contrasts. The ice cream is cinnamon flavoured but contains sour cream, which gives it an interesting tang.

Preheat the oven to 190°C (or 170°C for a fan-forced oven).

To make the ice cream, place the milk and cinnamon stick in a saucepan over medium heat and cook until just before boiling point. Place the egg yolks and sugar in a bowl and whisk to combine. While constantly whisking, slowly pour the hot milk over the eggs and stir until well combined. Return the mixture to the saucepan over medium heat and cook, stirring, until the mixture thickens and coats the back of a spoon. Remove from the heat, transfer to the bowl of an electric mixer and set over a bowl of iced water to cool. Once the mixture has cooled, remove the cinnamon stick, add the sour cream and whisk to combine. If it seems to be separated, blitz the mixture with a hand-held blender to bring it together again. Place the bowl back in the electric mixer and, while slowly whisking, add the liquid nitrogen and beat until the ice cream has set firmly. Alternatively, churn in an ice cream machine according to the manufacturer's instructions. Once firm, place the ice cream in a large piping bag with a plain 2 cm nozzle and pipe it into logs, about 10 cm long, onto a lined baking tray sprinkled with a quarter of the crushed freeze-dried apple. Sprinkle the top of the logs with the remaining crushed apple. Set aside in the freezer.

To make the pistachio cake, place the sugar and butter in the bowl of an electric mixer and beat them until light and fluffy. Add the ground pistachio nuts, ground almonds and salt and stir to combine. Add the eggs, one at a time, mixing well after each addition. Stir in the pistachio paste. Pour the mixture into a baking paper-lined 30 x 20 cm cake tin and bake until cooked through, about 25 minutes. The cake will be dense.

FENNEL SYRUP

1 tablespoon fennel seeds
100 g caster sugar
150 ml apple juice

PISTACHIO PRALINE

100 g caster sugar
50 g (1/3 cup) pistachio nuts

CARAMEL SAUCE

100 g caster sugar
150 ml pouring cream
1/2 teaspoon salt

APPLE CLOUD

35 g caster sugar
15 g (3 sheets) titanium-
    strength gelatine, softened
    in iced water
3 granny smith apples
pinch of citric acid
juice of 1/2 lemon

GARNISH

1/2 granny smith apple, peeled
    and cut into small dice
freeze-dried apple, chopped

While the cake is cooking, make the fennel syrup. Place all the ingredients in a saucepan over medium heat and allow to boil until reduced by half. Remove from the heat and set aside.

Once the cake is cooked, remove it from the oven and brush it with the fennel syrup. Cut the cake into 12 even rectangles. (Freeze the left-over cake and use it for another dessert.)

To make the pistachio praline, place the sugar and 1 tablespoon water in a saucepan over medium heat. Bring to the boil and cook, without stirring, until the caramel is dark golden in colour. Meanwhile spread the pistachio nuts on a sheet of baking paper. Once the sugar is ready, pour it over the nuts and set aside to cool. Once cool, break the praline into small pieces and set aside.

To make the caramel sauce, place the sugar and 1 tablespoon water in a saucepan over medium heat. Bring to the boil and cook, without stirring, until the caramel is a deep golden colour. Remove from the heat, add the cream and salt and stir until combined. Pour it into a bowl and set over an ice bath to cool.

To make the apple cloud, place the sugar and 35 ml water in a saucepan and bring to the boil over high heat to dissolve the sugar. Remove the pan from the heat, squeeze the water from the gelatine and add the gelatine to the pan. Stir to combine.

Juice the apples (you will need about 200 ml apple juice). Add the apple juice, citric acid and lemon juice to the syrup and stir to combine. Transfer to a bowl and set over another bowl of iced water to cool. When cool, transfer the mixture to an iSi gun (available at kitchen supply stores) and charge it 4 times. Set aside in the refrigerator. Alternatively, to make the apple cloud without an iSi gun, don't chill the mixture. Instead, close to serving time, put the mixture in the large bowl of an electric mixer and beat on high speed until thick and airy, about 10 minutes. Serve immediately.

To serve, place a slice of cake on each serving plate. Remove the ice cream from the freezer and place a log on top of each piece of cake. Drizzle with the caramel sauce and sprinkle with the pistachio praline. Remove the iSi gun from the refrigerator (if using), shake vigorously and squeeze a dollop of the apple cloud onto each plate (or scoop it from the mixing bowl). Garnish with the diced fresh and the freeze-dried apple.

DIGGIN' IN THE DIRT

SERVES 6

220 g dark chocolate, broken
  into pieces
1 egg
300 ml pouring cream
220 g white chocolate, broken
  into pieces
1 orange, segmented
18 raspberries
zest of 1 orange

ORANGE ICE
80 g (⅓ cup) caster sugar
juice of 2 oranges

ORANGE SUGAR
80 g (⅓ cup) caster sugar
thinly sliced peel of 2 oranges,
  pith removed

This is me on a plate. It's also about surprises. It might not look that exciting but, when you eat it, you find surprise after surprise. The orange ice, orange sugar and caramelised white chocolate are all hidden under chocolate soil, flavoured with szechuan peppercorns and popping candy. I've worked with a Bobcat in the soil since I left school, but I feel I'm also a bit of a surprise package. I'm not what people would expect. No one would expect someone like me to create a dish like this!

Preheat the oven to 180°C (or 160°C for a fan-forced oven).

To make the orange ice, put the sugar and 60 ml (¼ cup) water in a small saucepan over medium heat and cook until the sugar has dissolved. Remove the pan from the heat, add the orange juice and stir until combined. Strain the mixture and pour it into an 18 x 28 cm tray. The mixture should be about 1 cm thick. Place the tray in the freezer for about 2–3 hours, until set.

To make the orange sugar, place the sugar and 60 ml (¼ cup) water in a small saucepan over medium heat and stir to combine. Cook until the sugar dissolves. Add the orange peel strips and simmer until the caramel is golden, about 8–10 minutes. Pour onto a baking tray lined with baking paper and leave to set, about 20 minutes. Once set, chop it into 5 mm–1 cm chunks and set aside.

Put the dark chocolate in a bowl over a saucepan of gently simmering water and heat until just melted. Remove from the heat and allow to cool slightly. Add the egg and whisk to combine.

Meanwhile, put the cream in the bowl of an electric mixer and whisk until stiff peaks form. Reserve half the cream for serving. Add the

CHOCOLATE 'SOIL'

60 g (3 cups) tapioca maltodextrin

300 g milk chocolate, broken into pieces

1½ tablespoons szechuan peppercorns, crushed, plus extra to serve

50 g (¼ cup) popping candy

¼ teaspoon salt

remaining half to the dark chocolate mixture and fold it in to combine. Set aside.

Put the white chocolate on a baking tray lined with baking paper. Bake, stirring every 3 minutes, until the chocolate becomes a dark caramel colour, about 10–12 minutes. It will seem as if the chocolate has 'seized' when you stir it at 6 minutes, but don't worry as it will come back together. Remove it from the oven and spread it evenly in a thin layer. Transfer the tray to the refrigerator for the chocolate to cool and harden for about 20 minutes. When set, break the chocolate into 1 cm pieces and set aside.

To make the chocolate 'soil', put the tapioca maltodextrin in a food processor. Place the milk chocolate in a bowl over a saucepan of gently simmering water and heat until melted. Remove from the heat and add it to the food processor. Process until a crumble forms.

Transfer the milk chocolate crumble to a bowl, add the szechuan peppercorns, orange sugar, popping candy and salt and then stir to combine.

To serve, remove the orange ice from the freezer and break it into small pieces. Place a small pile in the centre of the serving plates.

Spoon the reserved whipped cream and the dark chocolate cream into 2 separate disposable piping bags, snip the ends off the bags and pipe dollops of both creams onto each plate. Add the orange segments, raspberries and white chocolate squares. Sprinkle with orange zest, then sprinkle over a few extra peppercorns. To finish, cover all the elements with a mound of chocolate 'soil'.

DESSERT

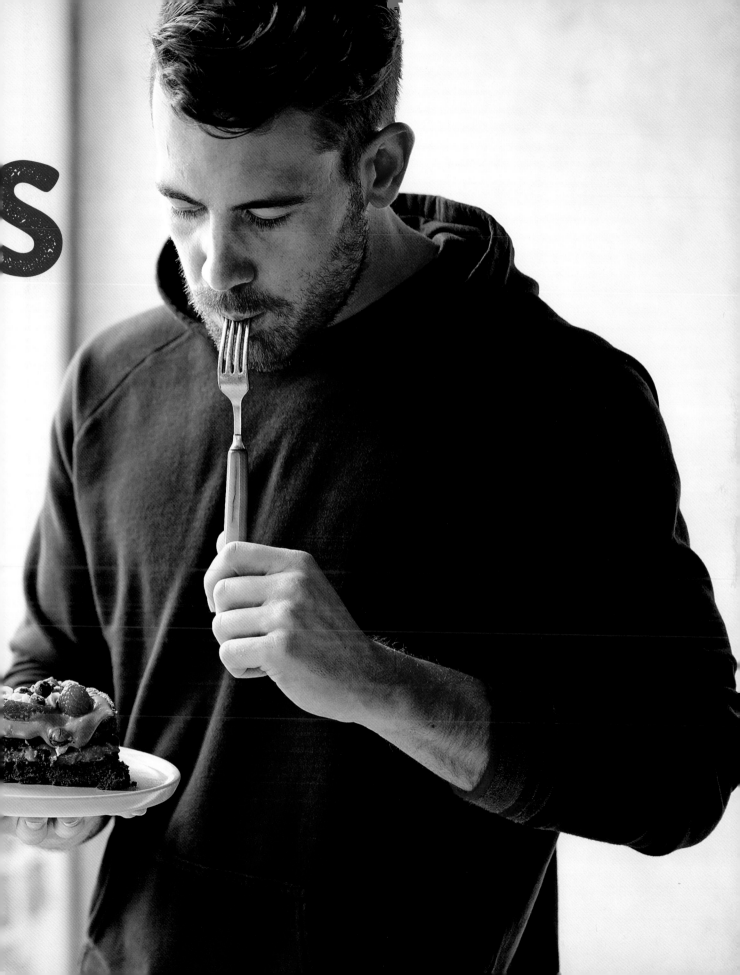

I've always loved eating desserts and sweet things but until recently I hardly ever made them and would usually just buy them. However, since going on *MasterChef*, desserts have become a main focus for me. I get more excited about sweet things now than I do about savoury dishes because, with desserts, you can incorporate unusual textures and ingredients, and that makes things interesting.

You can put a dessert in front of me that's been created by the greatest chef in the world, but chances are I'll go back to a chocolate brownie every time. I love all chocolate – I'm obsessed with it. I like it with hazelnut and orange as well as with more other unusual flavours like szechuan pepper. Caramelised white chocolate is a recent discovery of mine and, believe me, once you've tried it, you'll never go back to regular white chocolate again!

This chapter includes all my favourites, including mousses, slices, puddings, ice cream, cakes and crumbles. And, of course, there's a lot of chocolate…

ANZAC SLICE

MAKES 16 PIECES

150 g (1 cup) plain flour
175 g (1¾ cups) rolled oats
115 g (½ cup) firmly packed
    brown sugar
55 g (¼ cup) caster sugar
75 g (1 cup) dried apple, cut
    into small pieces
65 g (½ cup) dried cranberries
30 g (½ cup) shredded
    coconut
½ teaspoon mixed spice
150 g unsalted butter
90 g (¼ cup) golden syrup
1 teaspoon bicarbonate
    of soda

Here's a twist on an Australian classic - ANZAC biscuits. I love my ANZACs chewy, so reinventing them as a slice assures it will be soft. If you like, you can add other dried fruit, different nuts or flavours like cinnamon, clove or vanilla.

Preheat the oven to 200°C (or 180°C for a fan-forced oven).

Line the base and 2 long sides of a 20 x 30 cm slice tin with baking paper, extending the paper over the long sides, to assist with removing the slice from the tin when cooked.

In a bowl, put the flour, oats, sugars, dried fruits, coconut and mixed spice. Make a well in the centre.

In a small saucepan over medium heat, melt the butter and golden syrup. Remove the pan from the heat and add the bicarbonate of soda. Pour the wet ingredients into the dry ones and mix thoroughly to combine. Spoon into the prepared tin and press out evenly with the back of a spoon.

Bake in the oven for 15–20 minutes or until the edges are a nice golden colour and the centre just firm. Allow to cool in the tin for 10 minutes, then remove and cut into 16 even slices. Store in an airtight container for 4–5 days.

BRENT'S TIPS: I like my ANZAC slice a little bit chewy, but if you like yours crunchy, just cook it for 5 minutes longer.

You can turn this into a Kingston slice by drizzling it with melted dark chocolate once cooled.

BANANA BREAD
WITH CREAM CHEESE FROSTING

SERVES 10–12

225 g (1½ cups) self-raising
flour
165 g (¾ cup) firmly packed
brown sugar
190 g (1 cup) dark chocolate
chips
1 teaspoon bicarbonate
of soda
1 teaspoon ground cinnamon
½ teaspoon mixed spice
3 very ripe bananas, mashed
250 ml (1 cup) milk
100 g unsalted butter, melted,
plus extra for greasing
2 large eggs
1 teaspoon vanilla bean paste

CREAM CHEESE FROSTING
100 g cream cheese, softened
50 g butter, softened
150 g icing sugar, sifted
1 teaspoon vanilla bean paste

Banana bread was one of my mum's best recipes and she used to make this with very overripe bananas. The luscious cream cheese frosting takes it to another level.

Preheat the oven to 200°C (or 180°C for a fan-forced oven). Brush a 7 x 10.5 x 21 cm (1.6 litre capacity) loaf tin with melted butter and set aside. (You can also line it with baking paper if you're worried it might stick.)

Place the flour, brown sugar, chocolate chips, bicarbonate of soda and spices in a bowl and mix well to combine.

In a separate bowl, combine the mashed bananas, milk, butter, eggs and vanilla. Add this mixture to the flour mixture and stir until just combined. Pour into the prepared tin. Bake for 40–50 minutes or until a skewer comes out clean when inserted in the centre. Remove the banana bread from the tin after 5 minutes and set aside to cool on a wire rack.

For the cream cheese frosting, using an electric mixer, cream together all of the ingredients until really light and fluffy. Spread generously over the cooled banana bread or, spread on individual slices at serving time.

BRENT'S TIPS: For a less decadent loaf, leave out the chocolate chips and simply dust the loaf with icing sugar instead of the cream cheese frosting.

For a more nutritious loaf, add 50 g (½ cup) rolled oats or coconut flakes to the bread before baking.

For an extra spicy kick, add ½ teaspoon ground cinnamon and ½ teaspoon mixed spice to your cream cheese frosting.

EASIEST DARK CHOC MOUSSE

SERVES 4

150 g dark chocolate (at least
   70% cocoa solids)
1 egg, lightly beaten
150 ml pouring or whipping
   cream

This mousse is great for dinner parties. You can make it ahead of time and have it all portioned up in small serving glasses, ready to go for your guests.

Place the chocolate in a heatproof bowl over a saucepan of simmering water. Gently melt the chocolate and remove from the heat once it's almost melted. Let the chocolate cool for 2 minutes, then whisk in the egg.

In a separate bowl, whisk the cream to stiff peaks.

Fold the cream through the chocolate mixture then place in the refrigerator to chill and set, about 1 hour. Serve.

BRENT'S TIPS: If you want the mousse thinner, then fold through some extra whipped cream; and if you want it thicker, reduce the amount of cream you add.

A dusting of chilli powder adds a complex and interesting dimension to this simple mousse.

VARIATION
To make jaffa mousse, add the zest of 1 orange to the mixture.

SIMPLE VANILLA CUSTARD
ICE CREAM

MAKES ABOUT 1 LITRE

500 ml (2 cups) milk
500 ml (2 cups) pouring cream
1 vanilla bean, split and seeds
  scraped
6 egg yolks
55 g (¼ cup) caster sugar

I love ice cream. Once I discovered the custard recipe that was at the base and how easy it was, I went mad. I've never had an ice cream machine, so I just do it in the freezer, but an ice cream machine makes it really easy and also smoother. You can fold through nuts or chocolate bits or whatever you want. The sundaes are some of my favourite recipes in this book.

In a large saucepan over medium heat, bring the milk, cream and vanilla seeds and bean just to the boil, stirring occasionally. Remove the pan from the heat and set it aside to cool down for 2–3 minutes.

Meanwhile, in a separate large bowl, whisk the egg yolks and sugar until thick and pale. While whisking, slowly pour half of the slightly cooled milk and cream mixture into the egg and sugar mixture. Add the remainder of the mixture and give everything a good stir, then return all the mixture to the saucepan over low heat. Using a wooden spoon, stirring continuously, cook for a few minutes or until the mixture coats the back of a spoon. Don't let the mixture stay on the heat for too long or it will boil and split. Strain the mixture through a fine sieve, discard the vanilla bean, and set aside to cool in the refrigerator for 1–2 hours. The custard should be well chilled before churning.

To make the ice cream, churn the cooled mixture in an ice cream machine, following the manufacturer's instructions. Scoop into a 1 litre capacity container, cover and freeze until required.

If you don't have an ice cream machine, you can place the mixture in the freezer for 3 hours, removing it every hour and blitzing it with a hand-held blender or in a food processor and then returning it to the freezer until set.

BRENT'S TIP: If you don't have an ice cream maker and are freezing it, you don't have to blitz it, and it will still be ice cream, but the texture won't be as smooth. There will be large ice crystals through the mixture.

CHAI ICE CREAM

MAKES 1 LITRE

3 cinnamon sticks, crumbled
1 teaspoon cardamom pods,
   crushed
10 cloves
1 vanilla bean, split and seeds
   scraped
2 bags black tea
small grating of nutmeg

Prepare the simple vanilla custard ice cream on page 211, but add all these ingredients to the milk and cream mixture before heating.

Bring to the boil, remove from the heat and let infuse for 10–15 minutes.

Continue the instructions for the simple vanilla custard ice cream recipe, reheating the spiced milk mixture with the egg and sugar mixture, straining, discarding the solids, churning and freezing.

COFFEE ICE CREAM

MAKES 1 LITRE

20 g (¼ cup) coffee beans
2 tablespoons instant coffee

Preheat the oven to 200°C (or 180°C for a fan-forced oven).

Put the coffee beans on a baking tray and roast in the oven for 10 minutes. Remove from the oven, cool slightly and lightly crush using a mortar and pestle.

Prepare the simple vanilla custard ice cream on page 211, adding both the crushed coffee beans and the instant coffee to the milk and cream mixture before you bring it to the boil. Once at temperature, let the mixture infuse for 15 minutes.

Reheat the mixture and continue with the ice cream recipe on page 211. Strain the mixture before freezing.

PEANUT BRITTLE
ICE CREAM

MAKES ABOUT 1 LITRE

1 quantity Simple vanilla
  custard ice cream (page 211)
320 g (2 cups) unsalted
  roasted peanuts
460 g (2 cups) caster sugar
1 tablespoon glucose syrup
150 g butter, cubed
1 teaspoon bicarbonate of
  soda

Prepare the simple vanilla custard ice cream on page 211.

While the ice cream is setting, cook the peanuts in a dry frying pan over low heat until lightly coloured, about 2–3 minutes, shaking the pan often. Remove from the pan and spread in a single layer on a large baking tray lined with baking paper.

In a large saucepan over high heat, put the sugar, glucose and 60 ml (¼ cup) water. Once the sugar has melted, boil the mixture, without stirring, until it is a dark amber colour, about 10 minutes. Add the butter, 1 cube at a time, whisking until fully incorporated. Stir in the bicarbonate of soda – it will bubble up slightly.

Pour the mixture evenly over the peanuts on the tray and leave to set, about 30 minutes.

Once the peanut brittle has set, place it in a tea towel and smash it onto a work surface (or use a mortar and pestle), until the bits are roughly the size of a 10 cent piece.

Remove the ice cream from the freezer, and allow it to soften slightly if necessary, then fold through 1 cup of the peanut brittle. Sprinkle a little more brittle over the top of the ice cream. Place the ice cream back in the freezer to set until firm, 1–2 hours.

BRENT'S TIP: Store the left-over peanut brittle in an airtight container for 1–2 weeks.

ICECREAM VARIATIONS FROM LEFT TO RIGHT: CHAI ICE CREAM, PEANUT BRITTLE ICE CREAM, COFFEE ICE CREAM, POPCORN SUNDAE

DOUBLE CHOCOLATE SUNDAE
WITH HAZELNUTS

SERVES 4

70 g (½ cup) roasted
   hazelnuts
8 scoops Coffee ice cream
   (page 212)
60 g (½ cup) cocoa nibs

HOT FUDGE SAUCE
250 ml (1 cup) pouring cream
20 g butter
115 g (½ cup) firmly packed
   brown sugar
1 tablespoon golden syrup
200 g dark chocolate (at least
   70% cocoa solids), broken
   into pieces

Preheat the oven to 160°C (or 140°C for a fan-forced oven).

Put the hazelnuts on a baking tray and roast for 8–10 minutes or until aromatic and the skins start to loosen. Transfer the nuts to a clean tea towel and rub the hazelnuts in the towel carefully in your hands to remove most of the skins. Discard the skins and lightly crush the hazelnuts.

For the hot fudge sauce, in a large saucepan over medium heat, put the cream, butter, brown sugar and golden syrup. Let the mixture come to the boil, stirring frequently. Cook for 3–5 minutes until slightly thickened. Add the chocolate, remove the pan from the heat and whisk until melted and smooth. Set aside to cool slightly.

Assemble the sundae by placing layers of ice cream, hot fudge sauce, cocoa nibs and hazelnuts in serving bowls or glasses.

POPCORN SUNDAE

SERVES 4

1 tablespoon vegetable oil

1–2 tablespoons popcorn kernels

8 scoops Peanut brittle ice cream (page 213)

60 g peanut brittle, roughly chopped (see page 213)

2 tablespoons dark chocolate chips

CARAMEL

230 g (1 cup) caster sugar

250 ml (1 cup) pouring cream

20 g butter

½ teaspoon salt

Heat the vegetable oil in a medium saucepan over medium–high heat. Add the popcorn kernels, cover the pan and cook, shaking the pan occasionally, until all the popcorn has popped, about 2 minutes. Set aside.

For the caramel, put the sugar and 60 ml (¼ cup) water in a medium saucepan over medium–high heat and cook, without stirring, until the mixture is a dark amber colour, about 10 minutes. Add the cream, stirring, about one-third at a time. Stir in the butter and remove the pan from the heat. Add the salt and stir to combine. Set aside to let the caramel cool down to room temperature.

Warm the caramel slightly in a small pan over medium heat just before assembling and serving your sundaes.

To assemble, place layers of peanut brittle ice cream, popcorn, peanut brittle, chocolate chips and caramel in small wide glasses. Serve immediately.

APPLE, BERRY AND WALNUT CRUMBLE

WITH ICE CREAM

SERVES 4

5 granny smith apples, peeled and cored
300 g (2 cups) frozen mixed berries
55 g (¼ cup) caster sugar
1 teaspoon ground cinnamon
2 star anise, halved
75 g (½ cup) plain flour
50 g butter, cubed
100 g (1 cup) rolled oats
80 g (⅓ cup) firmly packed brown sugar
30 g (¼ cup) walnuts, crushed
cream or ice cream to serve

This is another classic that I love, perfect for cold winter nights. You can experiment and add different fruit combinations or different toppings. Frozen fruits are great to use because they hold moisture, which means you get more sauce in the dish.

Preheat the oven to 200°C (or 180°C for a fan-forced oven).

Cut the apples into bite-sized chunks. Combine the apples and frozen berries in four 250 ml (1 cup) capacity ramekins or a 1 litre (4 cup) capacity baking dish. Sprinkle over the caster sugar, cinnamon and star anise.

In a bowl, rub the flour and butter together with your fingertips until the mixture resembles fine breadcrumbs. Mix in the oats, brown sugar and crushed walnuts.

Sprinkle the crumble mixture on top of the prepared fruit and bake for 25–30 minutes for the ramekins or 35–40 minutes for the large dish, or until the fruit is tender and bubbling and the crumble is toasted and crisp.

Remove the star anise, and serve the crumble with cream or ice cream.

BRENT'S TIP: If the crumble is browning too quickly, you can cover the dish/es with foil.

RICH AND INDULGENT
LAYER CAKE

35 g (¼ cup) hazelnuts
240 g dark chocolate (at least
    70% cocoa solids), broken
    into pieces
250 g softened unsalted
    butter, plus extra for
    greasing
200 g caster sugar
4 large eggs
65 g plain flour, sifted
pinch of salt
250 g strawberries, hulled
    and halved
125 g blueberries
125 g (1 cup) raspberries
icing sugar to dust

CHOCOLATE–HAZELNUT
CREAM
165 g (½ cup) chocolate
    and hazelnut spread
250 ml (1 cup) whipping cream

This is almost a brownie...it's so rich. I have eaten so many of these cakes. I guarantee you'll make it again and again.

Preheat the oven to 160°C (or 140°C for a fan-forced oven). Butter the sides and line the base of two 20 cm shallow round cake tins. Put the hazelnuts on a baking tray and roast for 8–10 minutes or until aromatic and the skins start to loosen. Transfer the nuts to a clean tea towel and rub the nuts carefully to remove most of the skins. Discard the skins and lightly crush the hazelnuts. Increase the oven temperature to 200°C (or 180°C for a fan-forced oven).

Put the chocolate in a heatproof bowl and place it over a saucepan of simmering water. Gently melt the chocolate, then remove the bowl from the heat when the chocolate has almost melted. Cool slightly.

Cream the butter and caster sugar using an electric mixer on medium–high speed until well combined. Reduce the speed to medium and add the eggs one at a time, mixing to fully incorporate each egg before adding the next. Beat in the melted chocolate until fully incorporated. Fold in the sifted flour and salt with a spatula. Spoon the mixture into the prepared tins, spreading the mixture evenly, and bake in the oven for 6–8 minutes, until just firm on top and the mixture is starting to pull away from the sides of the tin. Remove the cakes from the oven and cool in the tins.

To make the chocolate–hazelnut cream, beat the chocolate and hazelnut spread and cream using an electric mixer until soft peaks form.

To assemble, place one cake on a serving plate and spread just over half of the chocolate–hazelnut cream over the cake. Place half the strawberries over the cream. Place half the blueberries and raspberries into the cracks and sprinkle over about half of the crushed hazelnuts. Add the second cake and repeat the process. Dust the cake with icing sugar and sprinkle over the remaining crushed nuts.

CARAMELISED WHITE CHOCOLATE AND BERRY TART

SERVES 8–10

500 g white chocolate
2 g (1 sheet) gold-strength
  gelatine
125 ml (½ cup) pouring cream
300 g frozen mixed berries
55 g (¼ cup) caster sugar
fresh blueberries to serve
fresh mint leaves to serve

SWEET SHORTCRUST PASTRY

250 g (1⅔ cups) plain flour
80 g (⅓ cup) caster sugar
pinch of salt
125 g cold unsalted butter,
  cubed
2 tablespoons iced water

I recently discovered how to caramelise white chocolate and now I do it all the time. It adds a whole new depth of flavour. This recipe also calls for making your own pastry. Give it a go as it's not that hard. Once you master this basic pastry recipe you can vary it to make savoury pastry or even chocolate pastry. See the tips at the end of the recipe.

To make the pastry, mix together the flour, caster sugar and salt in a large bowl until well incorporated.

Using your fingertips, rub in the butter until the mixture resembles fine breadcrumbs. If you can, work the mixture together using a food processor.

Add the iced water and bring the mixture together to form a dough. Roll the dough into a disc, cover with plastic wrap and put it in the refrigerator to rest for a minimum of 30 minutes and up to 2 hours.

Preheat the oven to 200°C (or 180°C for a fan-forced oven).

Once chilled, roll the pastry out between 2 sheets of baking paper, or on a lightly floured surface, to 3 mm thick. Line a 23 cm loose-based tart tin with the pastry, cover with baking paper and weight down with baking beads before blind baking for 12 minutes.

Remove the baking beads and baking paper and bake for a further 5–7 minutes or until the pastry shell is completely dry, lightly coloured and the edges are golden. Remove from the oven and set aside.

Reduce the oven to 160°C (or 140°C for a fan-forced oven).

Break up the chocolate and spread it in an even layer on a large baking tray lined with baking paper. Bake for 30–35 minutes, stirring every 5 minutes, until golden and a caramel colour.

Remove the chocolate from the oven and put it in a heatproof bowl over a saucepan of simmering water.

Put the gelatine sheet in a small bowl of cold water for 2–3 minutes then squeeze the gelatine dry.

Once the chocolate has completely re-melted, fold through the soaked gelatine and the cream.

Meanwhile, in a medium saucepan over medium heat, bring the frozen berries and sugar to the boil. Reduce the heat to low and cook, stirring occasionally, until the berries are thick and syrupy, about 15 minutes. Set aside and allow to cool.

Pour the berry mixture evenly over the bottom of the pre-baked tart shell. Pour over the white chocolate mixture and spread to coat the berries evenly. Place in the refrigerator to set for at least 1 hour before serving topped with the blueberries and mint leaves.

BRENT'S TIPS: It's important to blind bake pastry. If you don't do this the base of your pastry will be soggy and will collapse when serving.

Be careful not to overwork the butter and flour as the pastry will end up rather tough. Make sure the dough is rested for as long as possible to ensure the shell doesn't shrink as it bakes.

Use the best quality white chocolate you can buy for this recipe. Sometimes after you have re-melted the caramelised chocolate, the mixture may be a little grainy. Just strain it through a fine sieve and the mixture will be fine.

For a chocolate shortcrust, remove 2 tablespoons of the flour and replace with 2 tablespoons cocoa powder.

For a savoury pastry, remove the sugar and add a larger pinch of salt – adding 2 tablespoons grated parmesan with the flour is also delicious.

CARAMELISED WHITE
CHOCOLATE AND BERRY TART

MILLE-FEUILLE

3 sheets frozen store-bought butter puff pastry, partially thawed
6 small ripe bananas, peeled
115 g (½ cup) caster sugar
80 g (½ cup) unsalted roasted peanuts, crushed
icing sugar to dust

PEANUT BUTTER MOUSSE
125 ml (½ cup) whipping cream
200 g cream cheese, softened
140 g (½ cup) smooth peanut butter
1 tablespoon milk
60 g (½ cup) icing sugar, sifted

CHOCOLATE GANACHE
200 g dark chocolate (at least 70% cocoa solids)
200 ml pouring cream

In this recipe I've brought together chocolate, banana and peanuts to create a taste sensation. In one word – yum!

Preheat the oven to 200°C (or 180°C for a fan-forced oven). Line 1 or 2 large baking trays with baking paper. Cut the puff pastry sheets into 5 x 10 cm rectangles – you will need 18 pastry rectangles – and place them on the baking trays. Place another sheet of baking paper over the top and weight it down with another baking tray of a similar size. Bake in the oven for 10–12 minutes or until the pastry is crisp and golden.

For the peanut butter mousse, whisk the cream until soft peaks form. In a separate bowl, beat the cream cheese, peanut butter and milk until well combined. Add the icing sugar and beat until the mixture is smooth. Fold in the whipped cream, a third at a time, but don't overwork it. Transfer the mousse to a disposable piping bag, then place in the refrigerator to set for at least 1 hour. Snip off the end of the piping bag just before using.

For the chocolate ganache, break the chocolate up into small pieces and put it in a large bowl. Put the cream in a small saucepan over medium heat and bring to the boil. When boiling, pour the cream over the chocolate. Stir until the chocolate has melted and the mixture is well combined. Transfer to the refrigerator to cool – the mixture should be thick and able to hold peaks before you whip it. Once cooled, scoop the ganache into the bowl of an electric mixer and whisk on medium until the ganache is light and airy, about 1–2 minutes. Be careful not to overwhip or the mixture will become grainy. Put the ganache in a disposable piping bag. Snip off the end of the piping bag just before using.

Slice the bananas lengthways and then in half. Sprinkle the sugar over the cut surfaces and, using a blowtorch, caramelise the sugar, until golden. You can caramelise the sugar under a grill if you don't have a blowtorch.

Begin the construction of the mille-feuille in layers – there are 3 layers per serve. Start with a layer of puff pastry, then a layer of piped mousse and ganache, then top with crushed peanuts and 2 pieces of banana. Place another pastry layer on top and repeat the fillings. Top with a layer of pastry and a dusting of icing sugar.

PISTACHIO AND CRANBERRY BROWNIES

MAKES 12 BROWNIES

200 g unsalted butter, chopped

250 g dark chocolate (at least 70% cocoa solids), roughly chopped

5 eggs, lightly beaten

250 g caster sugar

200 g (1⅓ cups) plain flour

40 g (⅓ cup) cocoa powder

70 g (½ cup) dried cranberries, roughly chopped

75 g (½ cup) pistachio nuts, roughly chopped

Don't worry how gooey these are, because they are the ultimate - especially when warm! You get a tart burst from the cranberries and a crunch from the pistachio nuts.

Preheat the oven to 200°C (or 180°C for a fan-forced oven). Line the base and sides of an 18 x 28 cm brownie tin with baking paper, extending the paper up over the long sides of the tin for easy removal once cooked.

Melt the butter and chocolate in a medium saucepan over low heat. Set aside and allow to cool slightly. Whisk in the eggs until well incorporated, then add the remaining ingredients. Stir to combine. Pour the mixture into the brownie tin and bake for 25–30 minutes until the edges are dry and the centre is just slightly wobbly. Cool in the tin for 15 minutes before gently lifting the brownie out of the tin using the paper for assistance. Serve immediately if you like your brownie gooey or cool and enjoy later.

VARIATIONS

You can omit the cranberries and pistachio nuts and substitute 60 g (½ cup) walnuts and 60 g (½ cup) raisins with a splash of rum.

Omit the cranberries and pistachio nuts and use 125–150 g fresh or frozen fruit for a twist. Berries are great – just make sure they are completely defrosted and drained on paper towel if using frozen, as the extra moisture will affect the end result.

For triple chocolate brownies, add a couple of handfuls each of milk and white chocolate buttons and drizzle with some melted dark chocolate once the brownies are baked and cooled.

SPICED RICE PUDDING

8 cardamom pods, crushed
1 vanilla bean, split and seeds
  scraped
1 litre (4 cups) milk
220 g (1 cup) arborio rice
100 g caster sugar
50 g honey
Chai ice cream (page 212)
  to serve

This is an elegant, slightly Middle Eastern version of rice pudding. I've added cardamom but no other spices because it's served with the Chai ice cream. Using the arborio rice makes the pudding really creamy.

Put the crushed cardamom, vanilla bean and seeds and milk in a small saucepan over low heat and heat until the milk comes to a gentle simmer. Remove the pan from the heat and allow to infuse for 15 minutes.

Strain out the solids and add the rice to the milk. Bring to the boil, reduce the heat to low and cook, stirring often, for about 30 minutes, until the pudding has thickened and the rice is cooked through. Add the sugar and honey and stir well.

Spoon into ramekins for individual serves, or a larger dish for family-style presentation.

Serve warm with the chai ice cream.

BRENT'S TIPS: Stir through some sultanas when cooked, for some fresh bursts of flavour.

Don't add the sugar until the end of cooking as sugar retards the cooking of the rice.

You can dress this pudding up for a dinner party by sprinkling the top with 1 tablespoon caster sugar and caramelising it under a grill or with a blowtorch.

MOCHA CHOCOLATE AND HAZELNUT
SELF-SAUCING PUDDING

SERVES 6

50 g butter, melted, plus
  extra for greasing
150 g (1 cup) self-raising flour
110 g (½ cup) caster sugar
30 g (¼ cup) cocoa powder
50 g chopped hazelnuts
125 ml (½ cup) milk
1 egg, beaten
cream or ice cream to serve

MOCHA SAUCE
165 g (¾ cup) firmly packed
  brown sugar
2 tablespoons cocoa powder
1 tablespoon instant coffee
  powder
250 ml (1 cup) boiling water

This is an easy dessert and all the ingredients are probably in your cupboard right now. It's perfect for when you're craving something sweet and quick to make. I've added a twist with the inclusion of hazelnuts and coffee.

Preheat the oven to 200°C (or 180°C for a fan-forced oven). Butter a 1.5 litre (6 cup) capacity ovenproof dish.

Sift the flour, caster sugar and cocoa powder into a bowl. Stir in the hazelnuts.

In a separate small bowl, combine the milk, melted butter and egg then pour these wet ingredients into the dry ingredients. Mix to just combine and spoon into the prepared dish.

For the sauce, combine all the ingredients and gently pour the sauce over the pudding mixture.

Place the dish on a baking tray to catch any drips, and bake for 20–25 minutes or until the pudding is cooked through. Serve with cream or ice cream.

BRENT'S TIP: Put 150 g fresh or frozen berries in the base of the pudding dish before adding the pudding mixture. When baked, they will become part of the sauce.

INDEX

ACKNOWLEDGEMENTS

I love the fact that this hasn't just been a journey for me, but a journey for my loved ones too. Without them this whole experience wouldn't have happened – let alone be as amazing as it has been. Thank you to my beautiful partner, Madison, who pushed me into the whole *MasterChef* thing and who supported me from the get-go, through thick and thin. If you weren't around then I'd still be 'digging in the dirt'. Madison, I am forever in your debt now – thanks Babe! Love you. To Mamma, Pappa, sisters and in-laws and all my family, you are my rock, my support and my guidance. You are everything a person could want in a family. You have guided me through life, helped me turn from the dark side and blossom into the good. I love you all so much. Family is everything and I have an awesome one!

Of course, thanks to my second family from *MasterChef* – not only the contestants, but all of those who worked on the show too. I tried not to be a whingeing shit, and you were awesome in return! You are a top group of people, never to be forgotten and are now life-long friends. To those special people who helped me throughout the competition, I hope you receive everything you ever want in this world, because you deserve it.

To the awesome Hardie Grant team, you have been super supportive and super helpful from the get-go, always hounding me in the most positive way, and making sure I get things done. Kudos to all of you, friends, and I hope this isn't our last experience together!

And finally, thanks to you for reading this book, supporting me, believing in me and jumping on board to enjoy this life-changing experience with me! Without you, 4 am wake-ups Monday to Friday would still be consuming my life.

Published in 2014 by Hardie Grant Books

Hardie Grant Books (Australia)
Ground Floor, Building 1
658 Church Street
Richmond, Victoria 3121
www.hardiegrant.com.au

Hardie Grant Books (UK)
5th & 6th Floor
52–54 Southwark Street
London SE1 1RU
www.hardiegrant.co.uk

A Cataloguing-in-Publication entry is available from the catalogue of the National Library of Australia at www.nla.gov.au

Dig In!
ISBN 978 1 74270 966 6

Publishing Director: Paul McNally
Managing Editor: Lucy Heaver
Editor: Ariana Klepac
Design Manager: Mark Campbell
Designer: Kate Barraclough
Typesetter: Susanne Geppert
Photographer: Mark Roper
Stylist: Deborah Kaloper
Home Economist: Caroline Griffiths
Production Manager: Todd Rechner

Colour reproduction by Splitting Image Colour Studio
Printed in China by 1010 Printing International Limited

Find this book on **Cooked.**
cooked.com.au
cooked.co.uk